MANAGING DIFFICULT PEOPLE

A Survival Guide for Handling Any Employee

Marilyn Pincus

● ●

*With contributions from Bob Adams,
Michael S. Dobson, Richard Mintzer, John Riddle,
Gary R. McClain, and Deborah S. Romaine*

Adams Media
Avon, Massachusetts

Published by Adams Media, an F+W Publications Company
57 Littlefield Street
Avon, MA 02322

ISBN: 1-59337-186-1
Printed in Canada

J I H G F E D C B A

Library of Congress Cataloging-in-Publication Data
Pincus, Marilyn.
Managing difficult people / Marilyn Pincus.
p.   cm.
ISBN 1-59337-186-1
1. Problem employees. 2. Supervision of employees.
3. Personnel management. I. Title.

HF5549.5.E42P56 2005
658.3'045--dc22

2004013270

Contains material adapted and abridged from *Streetwise® Managing People: Lead Your Staff to Peak Performance* by Bob Adams, et al., ©1997, Adams Media Corporation; *Streetwise® Business Management: How to Organize, Market, and Finance Your Way to Business Success* by John Riddle, ©2001, Adams Media Corporation; *Streetwise® Project Management: How to Manage People, Processes, and Time to Achieve the Results You Need* by Michael S. Dobson, ©2003, Adams Media Corporation; *The Everything® Project Management Book: Tackle Any Project with Confidence and Get It Done on Time* by Richard Mintzer, ©2002, Adams Media Corporation; and *The Everything® Managing People Book: Quick and Easy Ways to Build, Motivate, and Nurture a First-Rate Team* by Gary R. McClain and Deborah S. Romaine, ©2002, Adams Media Corporation.

This publication is designed to provide accurate and authoritative information with regard to the subject matter covered. It is sold with the understanding that the publisher is not engaged in rendering legal, accounting, or other professional advice. If legal advice or other expert assistance is required, the services of a competent professional person should be sought.

—From a *Declaration of Principles* jointly adopted by a Committee of the American Bar Association and a Committee of Publishers and Associations

The people mentioned in all of the illustrations used in this book are fictitious. The stories are based upon predictable behaviors displayed by negative employees and the responses those behaviors received.

This book is available at quantity discounts for bulk purchases.
For information, please call 1-800-872-5627.

Visit our home page at *www.adamsmedia.com*

DEDICATION

This book is dedicated to my sister, Joan Beverly Gesang. She's a woman I admire and a great pal to me.

ACKNOWLEDGMENTS

Hats off to the hardworking men and women in our great country, the United States of America! And here's a special thanks to managers everywhere, who in their quest for excellence remain eternal students. A writer of books owes these managers a particular tribute.

CONTENTS

Part 2: Negaholics Exposed

Part 3: Communication: The Upside and the Downside

INTRODUCTION

MANAGING DIFFICULT PEOPLE is challenging, but it can be done!

Some people are a joy to work with and others are not. This is hardly an original observation. As a manager, however, you can't stand idly by and watch as difficult people disrupt your work environment, because it never favors business success. Quite the contrary is true. The antics difficult people pull are often enough to anger even the saints among us. Customers, clients, company executives, coworkers, vendors—anyone and everyone is a potential target for abuse. And abuse is not too strong a word.

So what makes problem employees think it's okay to behave in such destructive ways? After all, these people are collecting paychecks from the company, and you would think they would perform admirably, if for no other reason than to ensure their job security and keep those paychecks coming.

Many managers have pondered the motivations of difficult employees, and you'll find some explanations in the pages of this book. More importantly, though, you'll discover tips, strategies, and techniques for coping with difficult people, whether you can figure out their motivations or not.

You might be surprised to discover that some difficult people actually think their managers are the difficult ones. "Who, me?" you ask. "Nonsense." You might not realize you're being difficult, but virtually all the collected wisdom on the subject says this is likely. Remember, angry words and disruptive maneuvers only beget more of the same.

When a difficult person confronts a manager, often, the manager unknowingly becomes defensive. Let's say, for example, that a disgruntled employee storms into his manager's office and shouts, "Executives in this company don't care about people, they only care about money."

His manager might respond with something like: "We don't run this company for fun, we run it for profit. If we didn't, you and I wouldn't be here." As this exchange continues, voices rise and it's likely that blood pressures rise, too. Tension mounts, and round and round these two go. As the situation escalates, both manager and employee spout comments they'd never think of uttering under normal conditions. Each one considers the other insensitive, inflexible, stubborn, or worse. Voila—the manager earns a reputation for being a difficult person!

Now back up for a moment, to the point when the angry employee shouts, "Executives in this company don't care about people, they only care about money!" Things wouldn't spiral out of control if, instead of getting defensive, you as the manager say in a moderate tone of voice, "Jim, let's step into my office. We'll sit down together and you can tell me what makes you think so."

When you respond in such a manner, you're the one in control. You're a skilled communicator who knows how to deal with an employee like Jim. The customers listening to this exchange admire your response. Your response now stands in strong contrast to Jim's angry outburst and eviscerates his credibility.

This little book combines the best of what is already known about managing difficult people with practical, do-it-now strategies you'll use to get desired results. Practical strategies exist because people have basic needs and their responses to perceived challenges are predictable.

You'll need to customize some of your actions and responses to address the specific idiosyncrasies of particular employees. To help you zero in on particular issues and determine appropriate solutions, ten different types of difficult people are scrutinized in this book. These include:

1. The Bully

2. The Complainer or Whiner

3. The Procrastinator

4. The Know-It-All

5. The Silent Type

6. The Social Butterfly

7. The "No People Skills" Person

8. The Rookie

9. The Overly Sensitive Person

10. The Manipulator

Right now, you might be wrestling with challenges that one or more of these employee types presents. Entire chapters are devoted to each one, so if you recognize any of your employees in these descriptions, turn to the appropriate chapter to confirm your suspicions. If, for instance, you think that Jim is a complainer and whiner, then read that section and discover how to deal with him.

Have you considered that maybe Jim isn't a "go to" person? Or did you know that any expertise he possesses (computer operations, for instance) might be underutilized because coworkers and colleagues typically give a whiner a wide berth?

In addition to honing razor-sharp communication skills that will enable you to prevent or manage Jim's outbursts, you'll know more about what to expect and not expect from this sort of employee. It's a little like having a crystal ball at your disposal: You can "see" into the future. Consider the possibilities!

This is just one example of the valuable insights you'll gain by examining the various types of difficult employees and the problems they present. *Managing Difficult People* is laced with so much valuable information, it might be the last managing difficult people book you'll ever need to read.

1

NEGATIVE BEHAVIOR IN THE WORKPLACE

MANAGERS' ATTITUDES AFFECT EMPLOYEE PERFORMANCE

NEGATIVE EMPLOYEES AFFECT everyone around them with their "downer" attitudes. Their behavior poisons the work environment. No wonder absenteeism escalates, employee retention is seriously challenged, and productivity ratchets downward. And when customers are repeatedly subjected to negative employees, it's only a matter of time before they take their business elsewhere. Nothing favorable results from permitting negative employees to spew their cynicism into the office environment. Once you focus on how detrimental these people can be to your department's success you'll want to raise your antennae to detect this behavior with dispatch.

MAKING THE NECESSARY DISTINCTIONS

It's important to remember there are times when everyone—you included—behaves as though storm clouds are everywhere. Worries about an ailing parent, a friend's divorce, or a rebellious teenager can take the bounce out of anyone's step. Likewise, workplace challenges such as learning to operate a new computer program or tackling an assignment with different people sometimes impacts behavior. (These are the times when others think, "He's just not himself, lately.")

It takes an observant manager to make distinctions. You won't use the same strategies with employees who are going through a difficult period as you will with employees who are chronically difficult. That's not to say that some actions won't be recommended. Still, these folks will predictably return to "normal" when their concerns pass. The behavior of a truly negative employee is typical, however, and it won't change. At least not without good reason, and it behooves you to find a way to make that happen.

SETTING REALISTIC EXPECTATIONS

Beware of false expectations. As a manager, you're in the driver's seat and, like it or not, you're going to have to deal with problem employees. Take a hypothetical employee named Jones, for instance, who is a chronic pessimist. Maybe you keep telling yourself things like, "I'll figure out how to get Jones to see the glass is half-full," or "All he needs are some pats on the back. I'll send him a note and praise his work in front of others." Beware of making promises to yourself that you can't keep—you'll undermine your performance.

After repeated attempts to get Jones to drop his negative remarks and obnoxious behavior you might be ready to toss up your hands and surrender. Maybe if you ignore the problem, it will go away. So you tell yourself, "I can't give Jones and his nasty ways any more of my attention." This is certainly an option. But Jones won't change. If you think you can ignore him without suffering the consequences, you're entertaining false expectations.

Maybe the Jones problem won't be solved unless you fire him. That's an option, too, and it's discussed later in this book. But what if, for example, Jones and his actuarial skills are valuable to the organization? Or what if the Chairman of the Board, as a favor to someone, hired Jones? Technically speaking you can fire him, but practically speaking you've got to live with him.

If you map out a plan for dealing with Jones and don't count on overnight miracles, you're on solid ground. Can you map out a plan without obtaining new information? You might want to seek input from colleagues. You're probably going to plug in some strategies you'll find in this book. Help is available, and that's a comforting notion. Still, when you try something new and different you're heading into unknown territory and, thus, you are more vulnerable. Recognize that a trial-and-error period is necessary and you won't doubt your leadership abilities. Maintain reasonable expectations and keep your good humor intact.

This book offers tips, strategies, and methods you can use or adapt. At the same time, be on the lookout for additional material that supports you in this goal. (For example: *The Everything® Coaching and Mentoring Book* by Nicholas Nigro or *The Everything® Leadership Book* by Bob Adams.)

A Manager's Attitude Influences Outcome

Attitudes are contagious, so make sure you have one that's worth catching. Prepare yourself to manage for success:

• **Sustain a positive outlook.** Cultivate a can-do spirit, and you will be an inspiration to employees. And, when that's a tall order, fake it until you make it!

• **Be known as a fair person.** Employees want to be treated fairly, and you must take the necessary steps to make sure they feel that is the case.

• **Keep an eye on morale.** Morale at the workplace can be affected positively or negatively by an incident that, although it might seem insignificant to you, might be very important to your employees. A contented group of employees will do more and better work than an unhappy group.

• **Set an example.** If you want your employees to work hard and succeed, then set an example by doing so yourself. Be a spectacular role model!

• **Take responsibility for your actions.** If something goes wrong and it's your fault, step up to the plate and acknowledge whatever it is that went wrong and why.

• **Maintain your sense of humor.** Don't take yourself too seriously, and don't be in such a hurry that you haven't got time to tell or listen to a positive (tasteful) story. Studies suggest laughter and good humor go a long way in helping employees function well in the workplace.

• **Acknowledge good work through praise.** Everyone wants to hear "well done" now and then, so make sure you acknowledge good work. Say it privately and say it within earshot of others, too.

• **Give credit for ideas.** If one of your employees comes up with a great idea, by all means give that person the credit he or she deserves. Don't allow anyone to take an employee's idea and pass it off as his own. (Managers are sometimes accused of stealing an employee's idea; be scrupulous about avoiding even a hint of such a thing.)

Beyond the basic guidelines listed above, a good manager must possess other positive qualities:

- **Understanding:** Conventional wisdom dictates that you walk in someone else's shoes before you judge her. Keep that in mind when dealing with people in the workplace.

- **Good communication skills:** Keep your communication skills in good working order. You might want to join speaking organizations to learn how to be a better public speaker. But don't stop there. You communicate when you send a memo, write e-mail, and lead a meeting. There's no such thing as being a "perfect" communicator. An excellent manager will view the pursuit of this art as a work in progress.

- **Strong listening skills:** When was the last time you really listened to someone when he was talking to you? Did you give him your full, undivided attention, or was your mind thinking about five other different things? And when you are listening, do you really know what it is people are trying to tell you? (You might have to ask probing questions in order to get the message.)

- **Leadership:** Employees need good leaders to help guide them, so make sure your leadership skills are enviable and on-duty.

- **Common sense:** You'll need more than your fair share if you expect to be a good manager of people. Some managers toss common sense out the window and then foolishly wonder what happened when things go wrong.

- **Honesty:** Be honest and ethical in all of your business dealings—period!

- **A desire to encourage:** Encouragement is different than praise. Encouragement helps someone who hasn't yet achieved the goal. Employees need your input and

What's Your People Style?

Before you can analyze the personality styles and people skills of the employees you manage, you should first
learn a little bit about your own. Answer "yes" or "no" to
the following questions:

1. I enjoy meeting new people and am at ease in
   new social situations.

2. People tell me I have a great sense of humor.

3. I always look for the best in people.

4. I believe that attitude is important in everyone.

5. I lead by example.

6. People feel they can trust me.

7. I don't mind listening to people's problems.

8. I consider myself a fair supervisor.

9. People are a company's biggest and best asset.

10. People should always take responsibility for
    their actions.

If you answered "yes" to all ten statements, congratulations—you're probably an excellent "people person."
If you said "no" to four or more statements, then you
might need to brush up on your people skills. (Consider
attending seminars or reading more books on the topic.
Everyday Business Etiquette, 1st Books Library, Septem-
ber 2003, is one such recommended title.)

encouragement from time to time in order to be successful, so be prepared to fill that role.

• **An ability to delegate:** Be ready to give responsibility to others when necessary. Learn how to monitor progress without encroaching on their assignments.
Learn what you can from books, seminars, and other
resources that concentrate on the art of delegation.

• **Solid organizational skills:** While some people
thrive on chaos, most people prefer to work in an organized environment. Do you consider yourself organized?
If not, take necessary steps to fine-tune these skills.

• **Creativity:** Among other things, creativity will help
you to solve problems by coming up with more than one
solution to the same challenge. If at first you don't succeed, tweak your approach.

Managing people can be challenging, but at the same
time it can be fulfilling and rewarding, both for you and
for the company's bottom line.

The Power of Motivation

Motivation is a powerful tool when you know how to use
it properly. Have you ever given any thought to what actually motivates an employee to excel? In other words, why
do some employees seem as if they are always putting
in the extra effort, going the extra mile to get their jobs
done, while other employees barely scrape by? The reason employees—or any people, for that matter—behave
in a particular way is considered to be a *motive*. It's your
job to help provide motives for your employees to want to
do their very best.

MASLOW'S THEORY OF THE HIERARCHY OF NEEDS

Through the years, there have been many explanations as to what really motivates people. Psychologist Abraham Maslow developed one of the more popular theories. Maslow called it, his hierarchy of needs. He determined that when one level of a person's needs is satisfied, then the next level has the greatest influence on that person's behavior. This theory has helped many business owners and managers gain a better understanding of employees' workplace behavior. The levels are as follows:

• **Physiological needs must be met:** includes food, water, air, rest, and shelter.

• **Safety needs must be met:** includes protection from physical harm and freedom from fear of deprivation.

• **Social needs must be met:** includes friendships, affection, and acceptance.

• **Esteem needs must be met:** includes self-respect, respect of others, recognition, and achievement.

• **Self-actualization needs must be met:** includes a person's realization of individual potential, creative talents, and personal future fulfillment.

MEETING EMPLOYEES' NEEDS

If you were to use Maslow's theory, how would it compare to how you are meeting the needs of your employees? Let's look at each one and see how you can use them to help motivate your workers.

1. Hopefully, you are providing a working environment that meets all of your employees' physiological needs.

It doesn't take much to provide a cafeteria or lunchroom, along with adequate restroom facilities.

2. The safety issue is just basic common sense. If your employees can't feel safe at work, then you must be doing something wrong. Over the past few years there has been an increase in the number of workplace shootings and violence. Management should strive to make the workplace safe.

3. The social needs can be tricky. You want your employees to have a sense of social acceptance, but you don't want them to be socializing all of the time. Provide special times when socializing can take place. For example, plan a gathering to celebrate someone's birthday or wedding.

4. If people thrive with a sense of self-respect, recognition, and achievement, then it's your job to provide just that. Treat your employees with respect, let them know when they have done a good job, and reward them for their achievements, and they will return the favor by being loyal and working hard.

5. The self-actualization needs can also be easy for you to fulfill. When you see a person who is having difficulty performing his or her job, ask yourself: Does that person really have the skills and interest level required to be able to perform that task well? For example, if you have a payroll clerk who is having trouble working with numbers, but she seems to be a creative person, then move that person to a more creative position. Creative people cannot stand to work at the same job, day in and day out, all year round. A creative person who is forced to work in accounting is really like a fish out of water. Throw that person back into the pond, and let him or her experience the opportunity to be a loyal and hardworking employee.

OTHER MOTIVATIONAL FACTORS

Frederick Herzberg, another psychologist, also developed his own explanations as to what motivates employees. He suggested that satisfaction and dissatisfaction on the job come from two different sets of factors. One set is referred to as the "motivating" factors and the other set is called the "hygiene" factors.

The motivating factors include the following:

- Recognition

- Achievement

- Responsibility

- Opportunity for advancement

- The job itself

Herzberg theorized that those motivating factors were all related to internal satisfaction, and that they had the power to influence employees to improve their performance.

The hygiene factors include the following:

- Salary

- Company policies

- Working conditions

- Relationships with other employees

Herzberg speculated that the hygiene factors must be present in order to prevent job dissatisfaction, but that it is really the motivating factors that influence the employees to do the best job that they possibly can.

INCENTIVES AND REWARDS

As a manager, your job is to develop a work environment where the employee meets the needs of your business, and your business meets the needs of the employee. When that happens, a successful business environment results, and everyone is working toward the same common goal.

What can your company do to help your employees want to put forth their best effort? If you want to know what the majority of your employees feel would be a good incentive and reward, consider drafting a questionnaire. Keep it simple; just a few questions should give you the results for which you are looking. You will end up with a very good list to choose from to create an incentive and reward program that will work at your business.

Following is a list of some possible incentives and rewards (remember to involve your employees in discussions about any of these options):

- **Profit sharing:** There's nothing like good old-fashioned profit sharing to motivate employees to perform at their best. Come up with a profit sharing plan that works best for your company. Gather input from your employees. Ask people how they feel about such a plan, and ask them for their ideas to help make it succeed and benefit all concerned.

- **Time off:** There isn't an employee on the planet who isn't always looking forward to his next day off (with pay, that is). So why not build in some time off as a reward and incentive for doing well?

- **Trips to exotic locations:** People who work in sales for major corporations are used to these. Many big companies send their best salespeople on paid annual vacations, and those vacations are powerful motivators that encourage salespeople to do their best and excel at their jobs. You can probably come up with a plan that works for your budget and corporate culture.

• **Free merchandise:** Who doesn't like free stuff? It can be something that your own company produces or something from an outside vendor. There are plenty of companies that specialize in employee incentive plans by offering a wide variety of merchandise in their catalogs.

• **Employee of the month (or quarter):** Whatever works for your corporate culture, make sure you reward employees who excel above and beyond the call of duty with a special award. For example, you can reward the employee by giving him a prime parking space, listing an honorable mention in the company newsletter, or hanging a picture of her on the office wall. Some companies even offer extra time off for employees who receive an employee of the month award.

MONEY ISN'T EVERYTHING

Remember the old joke about money not being everything? Well, here's a real puzzle for you. To an employee, money isn't everything, but at the same time, money is everything. Confused? You should be, because any time you factor money into an equation that concerns employee motivation and satisfaction, confusion is bound to result.

Employees want to feel as if they are being adequately rewarded for the job they are performing for your company. But in addition to earning a fair hourly wage or salary, other factors are important to your employees. These include the following:

• **Pension plans:** Who doesn't worry about his or her financial future when reaching retirement age? Your employees are no exception, and many will seek out an employer who can offer a pension or retirement plan. Pension plans are subject to approval by the Internal Revenue Service since they represent a business expense, so make sure you're doing things by the book before you proceed. You can get information about pension plans from local banks and other financial institutions.

• **Health insurance:** These days, health insurance is a very important benefit, and the more you can help your employees afford it, the more loyal and hard working they might be. Small business owners can often provide health insurance without going broke. Make sure you compare several plans before choosing the right one for you and your employees. And when rates go up each year (as they most surely will), shop around and see if another health insurance company might be willing to work out a better deal with you in order to get your business.

• **Life insurance:** Life insurance is also an important benefit to many employees. Shop around and compare plans carefully before signing on the dotted line.

• **Tuition reimbursement:** Some executives believe it's important for their employees to be able to continue their education. As an incentive, consider refunding all or part of your employees' tuition when they finish courses successfully.

• **Paid vacations:** Let's face it, we all need a vacation at least once a year. And if that vacation is a paid one, then it becomes a real benefit and incentive for an employee to work toward making that goal become a reality. Some businesses offer paid vacations that are based on the length of service of the employee. Ask your employees for their input and see what they think.

• **Leave of absence:** In addition to complying with the Family Medical Leave Act, you might consider offering additional time off in the form of a leave of absence if special circumstances call for it. Survey your employees and seek their input on this potential incentive, too.

You'll have to confer with Human Resources and other experts in order to put most of these incentives to work at your company. When you survey employees or otherwise obtain their opinions and requests, let them know approval will be dependent on input from legal, accounting and insurance experts.

When you ask for someone's input, you owe the person the courtesy of a follow-up. What happened and why? If you don't plan to keep those lines of communication open, it's better to refrain from soliciting this kind of feedback.

If you pay close attention to your employees' needs, keep your expectations realistic, and exemplify the positive qualities of a good leader, it will go a long way toward keeping the majority of your staff on positive ground. In doing so, you'll also help yourself to deal with any troublesome negaholics who cross your path.

What's a "Negaholic," and Why Should I Care?

NEGATIVITY IN THE WORKPLACE is so prevalent, it's practically epidemic. In this book, the term "negaholic" is used to demonstrate the addictive aspect of negativity. This sort of negativity is dysfunctional, counterproductive, and contagious, yet to the negaholic it's strangely familiar. It's more comfortable for this individual to continue behaving badly than it is to consider the temporary pain of change. Like the common cold, negaholics can spread their "doom and gloom" about everything to anyone who is willing to listen or sympathize.

The Anatomy of a Negaholic

As a manager, you've probably seen your fair share of negaholics. Consider, for example, those negative people at staff meetings who seem to find fault with everything you suggest. "That won't work here," or, "Are you crazy? I'm not doing that!" they might say.

Certain characteristics are common among negative people:

• They usually keep to themselves. They rarely want to participate in group activities, and if they are forced to do so, the group's morale takes a nosedive.

• They often act selfishly and almost never consider another person's needs or wants.

• They never think a project will succeed, even if they're in charge.

• They have an "I can't" attitude instead of an "I can" attitude.

• They spend much of their time criticizing their employer and every business decision made.

• They might have a dysfunctional personal life and prefer that coworkers are miserable along with them. ("Misery loves company" is their motto.)

• They shy away from taking risks. Asking them to operate outside of their comfort zones is practically out of the question.

• They focus on the negatives, when everyone else looks on the bright side.

• They seek out "lose-lose" situations, instead of "win-win" situations.

• They tend to be secretive and avoid communicating with people whenever they can.

• They sometimes suffer from mood swings and are happy one minute yet miserable the next.

• They frequently take control of a situation and seek opportunities to make a mess of a project. When they succeed, they're quick to blame others for what happened.

• They are impulsive decision makers and usually make the wrong decision (sometimes on purpose).

Are You a Negaholic?

Negaholics don't earn accolades in the workplace and seldom climb high on the ladder of success. Before you attempt to steer your employees away from this destructive behavior do some self-examination by taking this short quiz.

1. Are you obsessed with negative thoughts about your job/company?

2. Do you have trouble with authority figures?

3. Are you determined to make people see everything "your way"?

4. Are you always looking for the bad in people, instead of the good?

5. Do you have trouble focusing on the whole project as a success, and instead look for little pockets of trouble?

6. Do you fret over world events and assume things will never get better?

7. Do you drift from job to job and anticipate more of the same in the future?

8. Do you look at a glass as half empty instead of half full?

9. Do you think of yourself as a "loser" instead of a "winner"?

10. Are you rarely happy?

If you answered "yes" to three or more of these questions, then you might also be a negaholic. This condition can sneak up on you! The good news is, you can change. The best news is that you're going to know a lot more about negaholics by the time you finish reading this book, and you'll learn how to manage them.

THE FINAL ANALYSIS

People are human, and humans are known for their unusual and difficult behavior. If you have an employee who is difficult, you can either transfer him or her to another department, or take the time to help this person become a happy, healthy, and productive employee. While the first option might sound tempting, you should opt for finding ways to modify and reshape behavior. It might seem like an insurmountable task, but when it is successfully completed you will feel a sense of accomplishment, and your employee will benefit immensely.

As you plan your course of action, here are some additional questions to ask yourself:

1. Is this person really being difficult? Before you make a big mistake, consider whether the person in question is truly a negaholic. Maybe she is just being difficult because she has a problem and doesn't know how to solve it. When people have problems, they sometimes lash out at their colleagues.

2. Can the problem be solved quietly? Sometimes it's just a matter of pulling the person aside and saying, "Hey, you need to get your act together because you're starting to be a real thorn in people's sides." If the situation can be handled "off the record," by all means, do so.

3. Does the problem really need your attention, or can someone else handle it? Perhaps a project leader or supervisor might be able to handle it for you. Just don't wait so long that the problem escalates further.

4. How can you help this person? While you might be tempted to give this negaholic a one-way ticket to Siberia, focus instead on past successes. Has this person been a team player up until now? Don't give up completely on a negaholic until you have tried several creative solutions to fix the problem.

Dealing with Ineffective Work Skills

Just as *too much* negativity is problematic and must be managed, so do other excesses need to be managed. It's often the person you identify as a negaholic who is guilty of excesses. Slow work pace, sloppiness, and tardiness, for example, are extremes that must be repaired. Continue your self-examination as you review specific excesses, but be assured you wouldn't be sitting in the driver's seat if you were "too" anything. Although the shortcomings mentioned above are spotlighted in the following sections, you can adapt the recommendations to other workplace excesses that need fixing, too.

Slow Pace

A slow work pace can be among the most difficult problems to resolve unless you have standards or goals against which to compare actual performance. For most nonprofessional positions, you can create standards or minimum quantitative measures of output. For example, warehouse workers may be expected to pack so many orders every day. Data entry people may have to process a certain number of entries each day. Salespeople may be expected to make so many calls to new accounts or close sales that add up to a set amount of revenue each day.

The work of professional employees, on the other hand, generally does not lend itself to quantitative performance standards. However, you can usually set specific time goals for the completion of projects. For example, you might require an accountant to accomplish month-end book closings within a three-day period or allow a software engineer two weeks to write a particular program.

If an employee doesn't measure up to a preset goal, the next step is a closed-door meeting with the employee. During this meeting, present the unembellished facts. For example, you might say, "You are packing ninety-three orders per average day, whereas our standard is one hundred thirty-five. How do you think you can increase your output?" Or, "Together we set a time frame of three days at month's end for closing our monthly accounting books. It is typically taking four. How can we work toward that original goal?" Make it clear that it's necessary to establish and honor these time goals for the sake of the company's success.

SLOPPINESS

Sloppiness is a common workplace problem. Examples include missing errors when proofreading company literature, omitting items when packing orders, entering shipping addresses incorrectly, and performing inaccurate accounting work. Sloppiness most often surfaces in clerical work, but it is also prevalent in the work of many professionals—although it is much more difficult to detect!

The first time you notice a minor incident of sloppiness, you should kindly point out the error to the employee. Don't comment, but watch the person's work more carefully.

If the problem persists or the mistakes are more serious, you need to sit down with the employee out of earshot of coworkers. Be positive, but be candid. Tell the employee you are concerned about the work and cite specific examples of sloppiness. Spotlight the clearest or most serious infractions. Avoid mentioning marginal problems.

Your goal should be to help an employee perform up to snuff, not to demoralize him or her. Encourage feedback, but expect to hear something like, "These are isolated examples. Everyone makes errors and basically my work is fine." At this point, don't get into a long discussion about how serious or representative the cited problems are. Instead, switch gears and tell the employee how important his or her work is to the company. Let the person know it's crucial to eliminate errors and sloppy work, no matter how infrequently they occur or how insignificant they seem. Try to end the meeting on a positive note.

Keep observing the employee's work. If, after a few days, work patterns improve, be sure to compliment the person. If sloppiness continues, conduct another closed-door meeting. In this second meeting make a judgmental statement such as, "I am concerned about the overall errors or sloppiness in your work." Again, bring up the most clear or flagrant examples.

For a nonprofessional or entry-level employee, assign someone with exemplary work habits that are especially strong in the employee's area of weakness to work side by side with the problem employee for a portion of each day. Ask the "monitoring" employee to suggest specific steps for achieving performance improvement. Personally monitor the work of a professional employee. Discuss any progress, or lack thereof, with the employee every few days. As long as this person has the basic skills necessary to perform effectively, sloppiness can be overcome in almost every case. It just takes a manager who is willing to invest time and who tries, no matter how frustrating it might be, to coach, rather than reprimand, the employee.

TARDINESS

Many good, hardworking people have a tendency to be habitually late.

Unless being precisely on time is crucially important, don't raise the issue with an employee who is occasionally late. Such employees will appreciate your tacit understanding and they will take it as a sign of your trust in them. Of course, if the employee is a security guard and you are operating a nuclear power plant, any display of tardiness could be serious. Use your judgment!

On the other hand, an employee who is habitually late can have a demoralizing effect on other employees who arrive for work on time. Furthermore, habitual lateness is an infectious disease. Soon many employees may exhibit tardy behavior. So where do you draw the line on tardiness? If a person is ten or more minutes late more than five times within a given month, it's time for a brief chat.

Assuming that the employee's job performance is satisfactory in all other respects, say something like, "Linda, overall I really enjoy having you on our team, but I would really appreciate it if you could cut back on your tardiness. I can understand being late on occasion for whatever reason, but enough is enough. Can I count on you for a little improvement in this area?"

Virtually all tardiness problems disappear after a gentle talk. But sooner or later you will encounter an employee who feels he or she shouldn't have to work on a schedule. Some employees might even be bold enough to tell a boss that "professionals" should be able to come and go within the workplace as they please. If you have employees who see nothing wrong with arriving two hours late, tell them that they can come and go whenever they please—just not at *your* workplace!

Post a "Pessimists Not Welcome" Sign

You are that sign! Your positive attitude and behavior can send the message that there's no need for negaholic tendencies in your office environment.

Remember that shortcomings and problems can almost always be overcome with some additional coaching or with a positive, but frank discussion of the issues at hand. You want to leave employees with the feeling that you are helping and supporting them, not reprimanding them. Avoid being patronizing and condescending— people are often not willing to reflect on things that are expressed negatively, and they may not react in a positive way when they feel they are being criticized.

If you're ready to set out on the road to repair problematic work skills, keep the following communication tips in mind.

1. Ask open-ended questions. Remember, your goal is to get enough information so you can work with the person to resolve problems and increase productivity. A yes/no (or closed) question will only elicit a yes/no response. A question that begins with "why" puts people on the defensive. Think about how you react when asked questions such as, "Why were you late?" or "Why do you act like that?"

2. Use who, what, where, and how questions to involve the other person. "What leads you to make that decision?" "How can we work together on solving this problem?" "Who else is affected when you're late?" "When do you think you can start working toward this new goal?" It takes practice to self-edit and reword your questioning techniques because people are typically conditioned to accuse and assume, not to accumulate information.

3. Be kind and courteous. Sooner or later you might win over even the most difficult employee with kindness. So instead of raising your blood pressure and losing sleep over "difficult" employees, kill them with kindness. That way everyone comes out a winner.

4. Match your words to your body language. If you're honest, your body language will confirm it. If you're feeling angry and denying it, your tone of voice might give you away. Be honest, then do a body check to make sure your words match your nonverbal gestures. Otherwise, your employees won't take you seriously.

5. Listen intently and avoid solving employees' problems. So often, our good intentions prompt us to provide solutions to people's problems when they don't actually want advice. Sometimes, people simply want to be heard. Comments such as, "That must be painful for you," "You sound angry," or "It seems like you're feeling frustrated," might seem weak and even ineffectual if you're used to communicating directly and giving orders. But the up-front investment is worth the results generated by listening. Once people feel genuinely heard, they'll entrust you with more information, which is what you want because it gives you control.

6. Invest a little time to figure out what makes someone tick. This isn't always possible, and you aren't a therapist. Still, some useful information might surface to help you nip a problem in the bud. How well do you really know this difficult individual? Some people feel like loners, and when things go wrong in their business or personal life, they have no one to turn to or talk with about their problems. If you invest the time, you might become this person's sounding board or even a mentor.

Remember, communication is a two-way street that involves sending and receiving signals. Empowered communicators learn to pick up on signals so they can be proactive rather than reactive with messages they convey. When communicating, pay close attention to the other person's body language, tone of voice, statements, and silences. And don't forget to put yourself in his or her shoes.

These skills will enable you to persuade your difficult employee to buy into your goals and objectives. Think of resolving these one-on-one situations as a dance. Until now, you and your difficult employee have been tripping each other up. Now you must take it upon yourself to lead, and hope that the employee decides to follow. If you bring an open, considerate, and skilled approach to all challenges, pessimists will get the message that they can't thrive or survive in your immediate environment.

Judging Situations Properly

In any situation, as part of a manager-employee relationship, the potential for a clash of motivations, fears, competencies, and communication styles is always present. For instance, you might be a direct communicator who takes action quickly, while an employee who reports to you might need time to weigh alternatives methodically before responding to your question. As a result of this difference in personality style, you might mislabel this employee as slow, incompetent, rigid, or difficult.

Remember, there are more viewpoints and approaches than just your own. As you become more attuned to your employees' personalities, work styles, motivations, and needs, you will be able to judge potentially negative situations better and set expectations that are realistic for each individual you manage.

One of the most rewarding aspects of managing a difficult situation successfully is cooperatively working toward a solution with a difficult employee. If an employee feels like a part of the solution rather than the source of the problem, it will motivate him or her to work with you to find solutions to problems without resorting to difficult behavior. Challenge yourself to learn all you can about listening empathetically, making nonjudgmental statements, and taking time to resolve conflicts in a win-win approach.

Your management skills will improve if you:

• **Learn as much about yourself as possible.** Recognize your own hot buttons: What is your threshold for tolerating different behavior patterns? Establish what motivates you and notice how it differs from your employees. For example, recognition for a job well done might motivate you, while the rewards of socializing might motivate an employee who works for you. Remember, it takes all types. What type are you? A driver? An influencer? A people-pleaser? A perfectionist? Be aware of the differences, and use them to create a more flexible working relationship between you and your employees.

• **Act assertively.** Assertive is not passive and not aggressive. It's simply communicating directly and appropriately. It means knowing what you want and thinking enough of yourself to say so. When you're honest and up-front with your words and actions, you're neither lying in an attempt to be overly nice and protective (in other words, passive), nor are you denying your anger to the point of blowing up some day (in other words, being aggressive). Asserting yourself allows you to hold your ground without putting the other person down, creating a win/win situation for both parties.

- **Don't try to solve a problem that is too tough to handle**. It won't always be possible for you to solve all of your employees' problems. Even if you're a terrific manager, that doesn't make you a therapist. Don't bite off more than you can chew—ask for help from executives who have more expertise than you do. If you've listened, asked caring questions, and involved the person in a possible solution, but you've still failed to reach a resolution, call in the troops: the human resources department, your company's employee assistance program, or your own manager.

- **Accept that you can't change others.** You can change your own behavior and hope that by serving as a model, employees will follow your lead. Do yourself a favor and understand that ultimately people do what they want to do despite your best wishes and intentions. Protect yourself by learning to deflect their negative behaviors, and don't take them personally. So often, out of self-defense and perhaps low self-esteem, we make false assumptions. It takes a self-assured person to dig in and ask constructive questions that lead to mutually satisfying results.

- **Remain flexible.** When you think about all the ways we are different as human beings, it's easier to understand that we view the world through different glasses. We are different in age and gender. Our upbringing, environment, education, values, and culture all define us in one way or another. Learn to accept the differences even if you don't agree or condone others' choices. Your life will be a lot less stressful!

• **Recognize when it's appropriate to say, "No."**
First, realize that what you really want to say is "yes" to yourself. Sometimes managers are so busy being caretakers and martyrs that they let their own needs get shelved. This is draining and ineffective. Learn to be emotionally honest. In other words, don't lie to yourself. Don't say or do something you don't mean. This is a particular challenge for new supervisors who are managing former peers and don't want to appear authoritative.

If you are having problems with a difficult employee, you need to make a careful assessment. Do you simply dislike the employee in question? Are the difficulties you are experiencing perhaps minor in character? If this is the case, drop the issue. If, however, an employee remains difficult despite all attempts at building rapport or providing help, and his or her behavior problems seriously disrupt the workplace, you need to take further action. (See Chapter 16: The Last Resort: Disciplinary Action and Termination.)

Assessing the Many
Different Behaviors

EVER WONDER WHY YOUR EMPLOYEES act the way they do? It should come as no surprise to you that because people are people, they all come with their own agendas. Some agendas will be proudly displayed, while others will be kept hidden.

Often, these agendas motivate people to act the way they do. Your job, then, as a super manager, is to take their agendas and make sure they mesh with your own company's agenda. You need to make sure that employees work toward a common goal. When everyone is busy with his or her own agenda, the only things that get taken care of are those things. Sometimes employees will do things that will absolutely drive you crazy, and you'll wonder why you ever hired them in the first place.

As you're juggling all of the various personalities and agendas in your office, try to think of yourself as an artist. Now, that might be a strange thing for a business manager to think about, but in reality, you are an artist who is in control of a business. As an artist, you *paint the right strokes on your canvas* to come up with the picture you envisioned at the start. You have the ability to create a successful business environment that will allow everyone to work together toward a common goal.

EXAMINING PERSONALITIES AND ANTICIPATING BEHAVIOR

The law of cause and effect tells us that for every action there is an equal and opposite reaction. The same rule can be applied to managing people. You only get back what you put in. As a manager, you can't expect to set things in motion and then sit back and watch things run themselves. It's up to you to put forth the time, energy, and consideration it takes to deal with the disparate needs of your staff members. Admittedly, this isn't always easy. Some people will be happy with the things you do and the decisions you make, some people will be sad. Some people will be cooperative, while some people will work against you. Some employees will be hard workers, and some will hardly work at all.

In Part 2 of this book, you will encounter the specific "types" of difficult employees. Within the *difficult people* category, for example, there's:

• **The bully:** This person can be hostile and angry, and won't hesitate to shout or throw a tantrum to get his or her way.

• **The complainer or whiner:** This person usually complains about everything and isn't interested in finding solutions. As soon as one problem is solved, the complainer starts to whine about something new.

• **The procrastinator:** This person puts things off often because he or she doesn't have a clue about how to proceed. The procrastinator typically has trouble making decisions.

And, as you'll see, the list continues. Chapters 4 through 13 each discuss one particular type of difficult person at length. It's useful to put each "type" under a microscope to identify characteristics that are unique to the type. If you know, for example, that Sean is a bully, and that a bully is hostile and might dump contents out of desk drawers and throw books across a room, you'll treat Sean differently than when you're dealing with another type. Bev might complain and whine, but you don't anticipate she'll act violently.

In short, when you scrutinize your employees' personalities and recognize which "type" they fall into, you have a better idea of what to expect. Then you'll be able to act or react with greater confidence. If, for example, Pete the procrastinator can't make decisions with ease, you'll know you need to partner Pete with someone who can.

GENERAL RULES APPLY

Even though each "type" comes complete with a separate instruction booklet, you don't have to memorize instructions. When you're familiar with the various types of negaholics you won't wake up one day and say to yourself . . . "Why me? Why do I have to manage this difficult person?" You can reach for specific information if and when you need it because you know it's readily available. (And, need it you shall, because these folks do show up!) General rules for dealing with difficult people apply, too. They're peppered throughout this book and might already be a part of your artist's palette/people-skills repertoire.

For example:

• **Talk to your employee about her attitude and try to figure out what the problem is.** Once she's aware that you noticed her bad attitude and poor job performance, she might try to curb it or correct it on her own. Believe it or not, often people really aren't aware of their actions or apparent bad attitudes until someone points them out.

• **Be sympathetic.** Let your negative employee know that you are concerned, while asserting that a bad attitude is unacceptable, and can be changed. People respond better to situations and problems when they don't feel so alone and misunderstood.

• **Ask for the person's input.** Sit down with a difficult employee and ask him how he can come up with a workable solution for the problem. Sometimes all it takes is for a person to realize that he's a valuable part of an organization, and that you do value his input. So don't forget to ask.

• **Offer a timeout.** A difficult situation might call for a timeout—for both of you. Often, a little space between you and the problem—and the employee and the problem—is exactly what's necessary. So use a timeout when you can.

• **Make use of what other managers know.** While you might want to avoid making point-blank comments and seemingly patronizing statements, you definitely want to have a good influence on all of your employees. Brainstorm with your colleagues about effective ways to educate and mold a problematic employee.

When "painting" with groups, you'll have to shift gears slightly:

• **Try to understand everyone's point of view.** Gather everyone together for a team meeting and ask each person how he or she feels the project is progressing.

- **Encourage participants to be completely honest.** "Now's the time to have your say while everyone is here to listen and has an opportunity to respond."

- **Address everyone's problems and concerns.** When concerns are put on the table, don't ignore them. Ask questions that force employees to come up with solutions. "How do you see this problem, and how do you think we can solve it?"

- **Keep lines of communication open.** Communication is the key to the success of any organization or project. Ask everyone how well they are getting along with other members of the team. Sometimes just having an opportunity to air differences can nip a problem in the bud.

In some instances, you might feel as if you're running as fast as you can but not getting anywhere. Maybe that's because you haven't stopped to consider some key behavioral traits. Be aware of the following points when sizing up workplace scenarios:

- **People are jealous.** Sometimes one employee might be jealous of another employee who recently received a promotion. Or it can even be unrelated to work. Maybe they are jealous of a coworker's new car.

- **They have low self-esteem.** Employees with behavior problems often have low self-esteem. They don't think they are worthy, and have a "why bother?" attitude when it comes time to doing anything, including their work.

- **They are critical of others.** Sometimes employees will make snap judgments without having all the pertinent information and they'll be too critical of everything and everyone in the workplace.

• **They are feeling guilty.** For some unknown reason, some employees who exhibit bad behavior feel guilty about something they have done in the past. Until they get over that feeling of guilt and move on with their lives, they will almost certainly have problems.

• **They are angry.** Many people have anger management problems and don't leave this side of themselves at home when they come to work. Short-tempered people are guaranteed to blow a fuse before long.

• **They are depressed.** Depression is a problem for many people. It's practically impossible for depressed individuals to be productive employees. Unless they seek treatment for their problems, don't expect things to get better.

• **They have health issues.** Unfortunately, people with health issues might have problems getting their work done. If an employee has a health problem, do what you can to assist him or her in getting help.

By now you might be putting your hands over your ears and closing your eyes! How is any one person supposed to deal with all of these truths, trials, and tribulations? Sure, it's a tall order, but it is possible if you stay proactive and come up with a workable plan of action.

SETTING EXCELLENT PERFORMANCE REVIEW OBJECTIVES

The first step to assessing any employee's personality traits and work skills is setting excellent performance review objectives. A performance review can be one of the most positive and proactive tools a manager can use to communicate effectively with employees. Yet most managers dread conducting reviews, and most employees fear receiving them. A major reason for these feelings is that many mangers don't know how to give useful reviews. Evaluations offer you the opportunity to provide feedback, direction, and leadership to your employees. Use these times wisely, and you'll reap the benefits many times over.

Using Reviews to Identify Personality Traits

Jim, a restaurant manager, thought of Irwin as the "silent type." Jim felt customers needed to be greeted and shown they were appreciated, and Irwin hardly said a word to them. After an official performance review, however, Jim realized that Irwin was actually an "overly sensitive" person. Once he figured this out, Jim took a completely different approach when encouraging Irwin to chat with customers. If Jim probed for information from Irwin in another kind of venue, he would have had to be more circumspect. In the course of a performance review, however, employees take it for granted that these sorts of questions are reasonable ones.

When preparing for and giving the actual review, keep in mind that your role as a manager is to guide the employee. Not only should you encourage and support the individual, but you must also coach him or her in the areas that need improvement. The employee should walk away from the review with a good feeling about his or her accomplishments as well as an understanding about what still must be done and how to do it. And, if this employee is one whom you consider to be a negaholic, you should gain more insight about what makes this person tick.

Careful preparation is key to conducting any useful review, but this is especially true when the employee is a negaholic. You'll want to be ready to work with the employee to set goals for the coming year, provide constructive feedback, and analyze strengths and weaknesses. If the review is objective and constructive, the employee will gain insight as to how his or her performance contributes to the company's mission, what the manager's expectations are, and what the areas are in which he or she excels and/or needs improvement.

Evaluating Job Requirements Objectively

Performance reviews are meant to help you objectively evaluate an employee's ability to do a specific job. You want to focus on issues that are relevant to the job and not on personal factors such as length of service or personal biases. Managers should also always beware of the "halo" effect: In other words, giving an employee a favorable rating for the year based predominantly upon performance during the previous month or so.

To ensure complete objectivity, managers must first understand the employee's job. A good way to gain this understanding is to review the job description with the employee prior to the evaluation. The manager can learn what the employee has actually been doing, what he or she likes and dislikes about the job, and what he or she wants to do in the future. This is also a good time to work with the employee to revise and update the job description to reflect current duties and responsibilities.

WHAT COMES NEXT?

Once you have the job description at hand and you've considered it, what then? First, you need to gather the following information:

- The employee's most recent job appraisal

- Reports, letters of commendation

- Complaints, warnings

You'll want to use these items as guideposts. Did the employee achieve the goals he or she set six months ago? Use measurable criteria to answer the question. If the previously established measurable criterion doesn't prove helpful, this is a good time to consider how to make it better. (You might not have time to accomplish this during the performance review. You can, however, set a deadline for retiring the old method and for introducing a new one.)

- **Examine notes maintained in the employee file.** Do the notes provide examples that back up criticism? For example, "You achieved your goal of revamping the process, but you stepped on a lot of toes along the way. You neglected to speak with Elaine in Operations and with the sales manager about how the change would affect them."

Do they provide reminders of special achievements? "Tom, I'm reminded that you served as chairman for the company Food Bank collection this year. I understand it was the most successful drive to date. This is something to be proud of."

- **When you write the appraisal, keep it short and to the point.** Remember, you or another manager will refer to it prior to the next performance review, so it should be specific rather than general. For example, "Tom met his goal," or "Tom didn't meet his goal."

• **Ask the employee to do a self-appraisal.** The employee should use a blank form that's exactly like the one you will use. It will be interesting to see if the two assessments mesh or don't mesh. If the employee's perception is very different from yours, you probably haven't done a good job of communicating with this person.

If you want to stimulate more employee involvement in performance reviews, try asking the following questions:

• What do you believe your major accomplishments have been this year?

• What could you have done better?

• What could I have done to make your job easier?

• What about your job would you like to change?

Finally, you'll set goals and objectives for the coming year and tell the employee where he or she stands compared to his or her last evaluation. Be prepared to discuss or not to discuss a salary increase. When you're seated across the desk from a negaholic, a salary increase might be the furthest thing from your mind, especially if you might be seriously considering the idea of firing this employee. (Make sure to read Chapter 16: The Last Resort: Disciplinary Action and Termination.) Just be prepared that even an employee you consider to be a negaholic is likely to ask for a salary increase.

When an employee's performance is below minimum acceptable levels in major areas, it's probably time to communicate clearly that performance must improve quickly and dramatically to allow for continued employment. You'll want to choose your words carefully and are well advised to confer with the company's legal expert before you call this employee in for a performance review.

DON'T FORGET TO GIVE YOURSELF A BREAK

When dealing with negaholics, remember to enlist all of your resources. Don't be unrealistic in your expectations about yourself. You can't be expected to shoulder the entire burden on your own, after all.

Success expert Zig Ziglar tells a story about a young boy that illustrates this point well. This boy went to see his father and said, "Dad, a tree fell down and it's blocking the path through the woods. I can't move it."

His father asked, "Son, did you use all your strength?"

"Well, maybe not," the boy admitted, and he went out to try again. Still, he came back saying, "Dad, I can't move the tree."

Again, his father asked, "Did you use all your strength?"

The boy thought harder, then said "maybe not" for a second time. This time, he went to the garage, got a block and tackle, set it up, and tried to move the tree. Then he went back to his father. "Dad, I *really* can't move the tree."

"Son, did you use all your strength?" his father repeated.

The boy thought hard, and finally said, "Yes, Dad, I did."

"No, you didn't," said his father. "If you used all your strength, you would have asked for help."

Remember, you don't have to rely only on yourself to solve problems. Learn when and how—and who—to ask for help.

NEGAHOLICS
EXPOSED

THE BULLY

A BULLY INTIMIDATES, torments and frightens other people. Tactics may vary, but results are the same. If you think you saw the last of bullies when you left school days behind, remember; bullies grow older and get jobs, too.

A bully can be male or female, large or small, young or old. Some workplace bullies target one or two coworkers with their obnoxious behavior. These cunning bullies act like wolves in sheep's clothing. Other people are surprised if they inadvertently witness this behavior since these perpetrators often try to pass themselves off as charmers.

Others are equal-opportunity bullies who aren't selective about their targets. These bullies shout at the boss, coworkers, vendors, customers, or anyone else when they're on a rampage. They shake fists, slam doors, and behave disruptively without a hint of embarrassment—or remorse.

Whether the workplace bully is a newcomer in a low or mid-level job, or a senior manager with years of employment at the company, one thing is for sure: When a bully is in your midst, trouble will not be far behind. It's important to identify and deal with workplace bullies if you want to have a harmonious, productive workplace. Office bullies are not only disruptive, insulting, and disrespectful; in extreme cases, workplace bullying can even lead to violence.

PREDICTABLE PATTERN

Bullies act narcissistically: "It's all about me."

Jane leaves her desk at 11:30 A.M. each day to go to lunch. One day, Delilah, Jane's comanager, asks her to change her lunch hour for the next few weeks. "The inventory figures will be faxed by the warehouse supervisors around 10:30 A.M. We need to have them posted before noon."

Jane's face turns crimson. "No one is going to die if they're posted later," she shouts. "You're such a goody, goody. Posted before noon," she spits out the three words as though they burn her mouth. "Maybe you should call your Mommy and get her permission to breathe." Jane storms out of the office and doesn't speak to Delilah when she returns.

The weekend intervenes but on Monday, when inventory figures start pouring into their shared office, Jane walks out the door precisely at 11:30 A.M. Delilah doesn't say a word about it. She has been on the receiving end of Jane's verbal attacks before. Each day Jane leaves at her usual time and Delilah hurries to meet the noontime deadline.

WHERE'S THE HARM?

a. Tension-related headaches and other maladies thrive in this conflict-charged environment. Consequently, absenteeism or tardiness is practically a "given."

b. Check-and-balance procedures are compromised when one does the job of two, so the risk for errors increases.

c. Internal and external customers hesitate to proceed with business in a hostile setting: Sales may be lost and productivity hampered.

RECOMMENDATIONS

1. Don't let every outburst draw you into battle. Ask yourself if a simple step can make the problem go away. Delilah asks the boss if figures can be posted by 1:00 P.M. instead of noon. When the boss says, "Yes," the challenge is removed.

2. Focus on a remedy. Select one that changes how the bully is impacted. Delilah tells Jane, "During these next inventory weeks, we'll take an extended coffee break just before the figures start coming into the office. That should make it easier to wait for lunch."

Delilah doesn't know that Jane needs to eat early because she must take medicine at specific intervals and can't take it on an empty stomach. Delilah isn't focused on "why," which she might never figure out. Delilah is focused on making a change that will affect Jane. When Jane agrees, the issue is defused.

3. Offer more than one remedy. Delilah asks Jane to choose one: "I'll do the posting alone. When you come back from lunch you can check my figures. If there's an error, it can be reported without delay. In exchange for this, you'll cover the office the last part of the day and I'll leave early. Or, if you want to work with me, we can have lunch at our desks at 11:30 A.M. Since we won't take our usual one hour for lunch, we'll both leave the office early. If the boss doesn't agree, we can take turns leaving early to make up for the short lunch breaks. You decide. Either way, it's okay with me."

4. Call for help! If Jane continues to rant, rave, and be abusive, Delilah's best recourse is to call for help. She may want to speak with their boss or talk to someone in the Human Resource department. If she prefers, she might ask for advice without mentioning Jane by name. If, however, Jane frequently makes Delilah's life miserable, she's well advised to proceed without invoking this courtesy!

UNACCEPTABLE ATTITUDE

Bullies appear to think highly of themselves: "How dare you question me!"

Howard rattles off information as though it's factual. A colleague has doubts. "Howard, according to the production sheet I'm holding, the figures for machine number twenty-two show twice the numbers you just gave us."

Howard pounds the conference table with his fist. "Jo-Ann, you have some nerve to question me!" he says in a low, guttural, voice while waving his pointed finger in front of her nose. "Your background in marketing hardly qualifies you to interpret production figures. I was a production chief when you were a snot-nosed little brat," he adds. "What's your problem Frank?" he asks when a third colleague shakes his head. Howard rises from his chair to show off his six-foot, four-inch height, and others seated at the table slouch in their chairs. He proceeds with the presentation, ignoring Jo-Ann's challenge. At the end of the meeting, he smiles, turns and extends his hand to her. When she reaches out to shake his hand, he holds her hand in a vise grip. He mutters in a quiet tone that only she hears, "If you know what's good for you, you won't pull that stunt on me again."

Jo-Ann is shaking when she returns to her office. She checks her figures and realizes Howard's figures are probably more recent. They could be accurate. "Maybe, maybe not," she ponders. "Still, his behavior toward me was outrageous."

WHERE'S THE HARM?

a. Howard's behavior toward Jo-Ann may qualify as harassment. At the very least, this bully purposely hurt her hand. Does this qualify as physical assault?

The head shaking, slouched postures, and deferential behavior exhibited by others at this meeting demonstrate that Howard's performance isn't unusual. By now, if you're the manager of a department like this, you know there's a bully in your midst. When faced with this type of confrontation, you must take action. The company could be held responsible if faced with a legal challenge.

b. If people fear intimidation, they won't be forthcoming when they uncover perceived errors or have additional information to contribute to a discussion. Quality control is at risk and other company standards may be gutted when no one is minding the store!

RECOMMENDATIONS

1. Seek legal advice. When dealing with someone like Howard, it helps to jot down his words and make note of his deeds. If you were there in this meeting and witnessed Howard's behavior, you should note the vindictive handshake, for example, while it's fresh in your mind. Does Howard's behavior constitute sexual discrimination or abuse? You may have to notify a senior company executive in order to approach the company's legal expert. Company executives will be advised to be proactive. They may require Howard to attend sensitivity training or some company-sponsored behavior modification program.

If you didn't witness such behavior and instead, Jo-Ann notified you, her supervisor, of the incident after it occurred, you need to make it clear that this type of behavior will not be tolerated. Howard's brand of bullying could be a prelude to even worse behavior, so you must curb it before the problem escalates.

2. Pay a group visit. There's power in numbers, and a bully might not act like such a bully when you have other staff members there with you for back up. Talk to the bully about how his or her actions make everyone feel, so he or she knows the negative behavior is impacting your department as a whole. "The way you treated Jo-Ann made us all feel uncomfortable." And, "You didn't ask Jo-Ann where she got her figures or discuss why there is a discrepancy. How can we feel confident that the figures we're working with are accurate?"

3. Deliver a warning (show-and-tell time). As a manager, you need to tell Howard in no uncertain terms that his behavior toward Jo-Ann was out of line. Show him written company policy that addresses code of conduct. (Sometimes a company mission statement covers the topic.) If you currently don't have a code of conduct policy in writing, create one yourself, or work with Human Resource management to accomplish this goal. Let Howard know you're taking steps to ensure that an incident like this isn't repeated.

Be forewarned. Howard demonstrated aggressive behavior when he belittled Jo-Ann, acted condescendingly, and squeezed her hand. You may be putting yourself at risk if you confront him alone. Even though you're the manager, you still need to protect yourself. Back-up is in order here: Tell someone you plan to confront him, and let Howard know others know you're meeting with him about this issue.

Sneaky Scheme

Bullies use the silent treatment and other antisocial tricks to call the shots.

Gretchen rarely returns her colleagues' phone calls. Whenever she feels like it, she walks in and interrupts them. Sometimes she just glares at people and remains silent. Occasionally, she turns on her heel and walks out when the other person is speaking. She behaves as though she's angry and it's everyone else's fault.

Where's the Harm?

a. Gretchen's tactics dominate personal interactions. People who deal with Gretchen walk on eggshells. They waste time and energy that should be spent doing their work. Productivity suffers.

b. Mutual trust is eroded and cooperation isn't possible. It's not likely that anyone asks Gretchen for backup or support. Her value to the company is diminished since she isn't trusted and certainly isn't a team player.

Recommendations

1. Question all rude behavior. Gretchen may be the wrong person for the job. Monitor her performance carefully and document your observations. Your notes should address specifics. For example: Omitted New Jersey figures in monthly report. Missing figures for six retail stores skewed conclusions.

Eventually, you'll have an objective picture to use to decide whether she goes or stays in your department. Gretchen's behavior may change if she works at a job she is able to perform.

On the chance that her job performance is excellent, arrange to have a private talk with her. Let her know that she needs to develop productive people skills. Invite her to design a plan to meet this goal. Make suggestions and do what you can to assist.

2. Match training opportunities to needs. If you're in the habit of ignoring announcements of seminars coming to your locale, don't! Gretchen might benefit from attending a Business Etiquette Seminar. If you send her to one, it might alert her that you're displeased with her lack of good manners. Seminars are only one type of training opportunity. Take advantage of newsletter subscriptions, guest speakers, and any other tools that can teach your employees to perform without resorting to bully-like ways.

3. Clap your hands. When the bully shows signs of improvement, acknowledge the change. A few kind, sincere words should make an impact. "I like the way you came up with suggestions at the meeting today. And I appreciated it when you didn't interrupt Roberts, even though he frequently repeated himself." Or, "Frank Jones told me the new customer was rude but that you took it all in stride and got the order anyway. Nice going!"

In a Word . . .

Don't worry about *why* a bully is manipulative, lies to you, acts narcissistically, is emotionally cold, and so on. That's probably a job for a psychiatrist. And don't plan to change the bully in some profound way. Your job is to keep the workplace free from the *unacceptable* behavior a bully brings to it. Some office and workplace infractions don't warrant your immediate attention; this one does. The moment you're aware that someone intimidates, torments, and frightens others is the moment you must act. If necessary, ask your own supervisor for help, and "manage" the office bully until office harmony is restored and no one feels threatened. Anything less is unacceptable!

THE COMPLAINER
OR WHINER

THIS PERSON GROUCHES and groans and makes it seem like an hour doesn't pass without something horrible happening. And yet, he or she rarely, if ever, makes a suggestion that might serve to remedy the alleged problem.

The complainer or whiner isn't content unless sharing dire observations with others. As a result, coworkers are kept from their work while they take time to listen.

Do these first two paragraphs put *you* in a positive frame of mind? They do not! Neither does the complainer or whiner put *anyone* in a positive frame of mind.

The atmosphere is charged with negativity when a complainer holds court. When coworkers tire of this, they might get into the habit of ignoring this individual. If you know the story of the boy who cried "Wolf," you know this is a worrisome situation. On the chance the complainer unearths something of value to complain about, coworkers and managers are inclined to ignore it.

Why doesn't this individual see the glass as half full instead of practically empty? Maybe he or she is just a generally pessimistic person; or maybe there is something specific going on in his or her life that has prompted such gloom and doom. Whatever the case may be, don't spend time chasing answers, because the health of your company doesn't rise or fall on this issue. Give "reforming" a complainer a low priority on your schedule of things to do.

Anyone who lives with a chronic complainer, however, will tell you that over the long haul this person's behavior irritates everyone. That's not a pleasant prospect. And, if you're intent on building a team of winners, the complainer doesn't complement the group.

Predictable Pattern

Complainers are not doers:
"It's terrible. Somebody better fix it."

Franco is a chronic complainer. For the last two weeks, he's complained about the office coffee. "This stuff isn't fit for human consumption," he announces each morning as he exits the employee lounge with a coffee mug in his hand. He hangs around Ginger's desk as he sips coffee and gripes.

By the time week three rolls around, Ginger is ready for him. "Franco, we have a new coffee pot. As of today, we're brewing a premium coffee using freshly ground beans and filtered water. The coffee is excellent."

Franco looks surprised. He sips his coffee and says, "Coffee isn't good for us anyway. Why isn't there any green tea in the lounge? And the chairs in there are so uncomfortable. They have no business calling it a lounge." Ginger smiles but when she looks at Franco, he isn't smiling. He's serious.

Where's the Harm?

a. People lose respect for a chronic complainer/whiner. This individual won't ever be a "go to" person. Consequently, any expertise the complainer possesses (maybe he's great at computer operations, for instance) will be underutilized. Coworkers and colleagues typically give a whiner a wide berth.

b. When things are difficult (for example, rumor has it the company is being sold), this individual adds fuel to the fire. It's easier to tolerate negativity when everything is going well. In rough times, however, two or three chronic complainers can do as much damage to your office environment as an invading army. The already dicey scene is peppered with their intense negativity and morale sinks to new lows.

RECOMMENDATIONS

1. Listen. Complainers may be dramatic, over-the-top types but they frequently point out things that are otherwise overlooked. It's reasonable to expect a good cup of coffee to be available in the employee lounge. Ginger deals with the coffee vendor and when she lodges a complaint, the vendor remedies the situation. She isn't a coffee drinker and takes action based upon Franco's complaints.

2. Model the opposite behavior when you're with a complainer. Whenever Franco stops at Ginger's station, she says at least three positive things. "I like your tie," or "Isn't the weather gorgeous?" or "I can't wait to attend the industry tradeshow. It'll be fun." Her comments don't change Franco's whining ways but they deflect his negativity. She even enjoys the challenge of having at least three, new and positive, things to say whenever he approaches.

3. Don't be forced into making a comment. Ginger can tell Franco she will talk to the coffee vendor but she doesn't have to say anything else in response.

Even when Franco pauses waiting for her to say something, she can change the subject or remain silent. Some
people are uncomfortable with dead air (i.e., an unexpected quiet period that would otherwise be filled with
talk), but if you refuse to be coerced, don't respond. A
complainer or whiner gets bored without the give-and-
take, gives up, and moves on.

UNACCEPTABLE ATTITUDE

**Whiners think, "I'm permitted to be loud and
interrupt. Good manners can wait."**

Richard is a well-mannered man when he isn't complaining. But twice or more each day he sets a good example
of what *not* to do in the charm department. He interrupts
conversations, opens closed doors without knocking,
and walks out of the room while someone is still speaking to him.

"The mail is stalled in the mailroom," he shouts.
"The contract was supposed to be sent via Express Mail
and no one sent it out—period." He paces in front of his
supervisor's desk stopping only to pound on the desktop
to emphasize the word "was."

The supervisor says, "Sit down, Richard. I need to
speak with you now."

WHERE'S THE HARM?

a. Rude behavior indicates a breakdown in communication. Good manners and appropriate business
etiquette support strong communication, and strong
communication supports business success. Richard may
have a bona fide gripe, but nothing will happen to change
conditions if he can't communicate with his supervisor.
When he invades her personal space and startles her out

of her budget forecasting reverie, for example, real-issue communication is delayed.

b. Clarity can get lost in the noise. Listeners are distracted by a messenger's abrasive delivery. They hear the messages but don't get the full impact of the meanings. In Richard's case, the Express Mail should be arranged for immediately. Instead, his supervisor tells him to sit down. She's going to talk to him.

RECOMMENDATIONS

1. Insist on proper business etiquette at all times. Set high standards for good manners, and demonstrate your respect for staff members and colleagues by maintaining impeccable manners yourself. Even a complainer who has good reason to be provoked will be unaccustomed to rude behavior in the workplace. It won't occur to him to be rude. Agitated? Yes. Rude and disruptive? No.

2. Run a tight ship. If someone in the mailroom is responsible for the delay in mailing an important contract, what else is happening in the mailroom? It's easy to be diverted by Richard's outrage and the problem at hand, but it's important to dig deeper. And, for a true display of courtesy, ask the mailroom manager to put it in writing for you once the contract is mailed, and then copy Richard as well. If mailroom procedures need tweaking to prevent delays, don't dismiss the issue until those procedures are in-place. In short, don't drop the ball now. Your response to Richard's complaint might take more than slap-dash measures, but in the end, your efforts should prove worthwhile because you'll oversee a more efficient operation.

SNEAKY SCHEME

Complainers suck the air out of the room: "All eyes on me, folks."

Morgan corners coworkers in the elevator each morning. These people serve as captive audiences, and she takes advantage of it. "Would you believe what the dry cleaner did to my skirt?" she whines, waiting for someone to acknowledge her. When no one speaks she asks, "Francis, who is your dry cleaner?" Francis answers. And then Morgan ratchets up her complaints another notch. "Well, if I weren't supporting my sick aunt, I'd have money for the kind of quality dry cleaner you use," she offers to all assembled.

Later, when people are in the employee lunchroom, she strikes again. "I'm sick to death of carrot sticks. I eat rabbit food so I'll look good for Carl. Do you think Carl cares? I was dressed up for our Saturday night date and he wore blue jeans." Morgan waits for a response and when she doesn't get one, she turns to Bill. "Bill, do you wear blue jeans on dates?"

Bill winks and says, "I like carrot sticks, Morgan. Pass them to me if you don't want them."

WHERE'S THE HARM?

a. People can't relax in the presence of a whiner. When employees spend eight hours a day, five days a week together, it's natural to share some downtime, too. The whiner makes it necessary for people to be on guard. When that happens, downtime isn't used for rest and renewal. Even a trip to the water cooler, which should be an opportunity to stretch and refresh, is undermined if the whiner springs into action. As a result, overall productivity gets a kick in the shins.

b. One person simply isn't available to respond to business needs. The whiner is so me-focused he or she doesn't hone in on anything else with objectivity. This individual doesn't have the skills to empathize with customers, clients, or coworkers. Since the whiner is unavailable to handle situations that require "consideration for the other person's needs," you're sometimes stuck operating with one less person on your staff. The payroll department writes checks for fifteen individuals but only fourteen employees are functioning to full potential!

RECOMMENDATIONS

1. Don't take it personally. Bill didn't bother to respond to Morgan's blue jeans question. He could have taken offense, thinking that Morgan was singling him out or questioning his good judgment. At the same time, he wasn't rude. Anyone within earshot probably smiled at his request for Morgan's carrot sticks.

2. Introduce a topic for discussion. If you're quick to start a discussion, the complainer is preempted. When the whiner gets onto the elevator in the morning, if you say something like: "How about those Red Sox?" the conversation is off and running before the complainer can blink an eye. Even if the whiner gets a jump on you and is already complaining about the dry cleaner, there's no reason why you can't introduce another topic for discussion.

3. Agree with the whiner and move on. Tell Morgan, "It's true the cost of living is high and I have to stay within a careful budget, too. But I figure it's worth the price to have a good dry cleaner." Or, tell her you're tired of carrot sticks, too. You might also toss her a what-do-you-think question, as in: "What do you think of the newly decorated reception area?" or "What do you think of the new bus routes?"

Then be ready for complaints. "I hate the new bus routes. They make my ride to work ten minutes longer!" In that case, after her response, simply move on. "I've got a call to make, Morgan. I've got to go." Eventually, the whiner might notice he or she doesn't get any sympathy from you, and you're usually too busy to chat for any length of time. It's a helpful message to send. Remember, you're not out to try to change these individuals, you just want to prevent them from disrupting your office environment.

4. Make it the complainer's responsibility. A question that requires the complainer to come up with a solution is warranted immediately after the complaint is registered. When the complainer grumbles that "The chairs in the employee's lounge are so uncomfortable, I stand up when I take my break," you should ask, "What do you suggest?" Then listen carefully to the response. If you need to ask other questions, do so. End the exchange by asking the whiner to "put it in writing." Request that it be delivered to your office. You'll have the responsibility of replying, but the complainer might not be so quick to approach you with complaints if it leads to work on his part. Or, he might think more carefully next time before speaking out.

In a Word . . .

Spending time with chronic complainers will never be at the top of your Things-I-Love-to-Do List. Even though these individuals won't sink your ship once you realize how to out-maneuver them, you're well advised to stay away from them. Since that might not always be possible, however, spend as little time as you can with these negative people. And spare the rest of your staff, too. Keep this in mind when you plan group assignments. Never partner the complainer with a group of mild-mannered employees. They automatically become a captive audience and are likely to experience a meltdown. Upbeat, outspoken types can better endure the whiner, but it's better still if no one has to *endure*. If you sense signs of these personality types in the interview process, don't hire them!

THE PROCRASTINATOR

LOOK IN THE MIRROR. Do you see a procrastinator? It's human nature to delay, stall, and put off acting for a variety of reasons from time to time. You might find a task boring, or you might not be sure what's expected of you. If you tend to be a perfectionist, you also might delay things because you're not sure if you can live up to expectations—your own or others'. Occasionally, it's a matter of time management, with too many tasks vying for your attention. "I'll get to that later, but right now, I have to do this," you think. And so it goes.

A *chronic* procrastinator almost always asks for more time to complete a task, however. You can't depend on this employee to meet deadlines. Business operations that require a series of tasks to be completed by more than one person are always problematic when a procrastinator is in the group. Productivity suffers and something more insidious is afoot. Workplace harmony is repeatedly undermined. Other employees who consistently step in to assist and pick up the pace have every right to be resentful. They complete their own job tasks and then do more. The procrastinator, on the other hand, doesn't complete his or her own job and is rarely available to do more.

The rhythm of everyday give and take is out of sync because the procrastinator, in effect, is a slacker.

You might not be a proponent of micromanagement, but you might have to resort to a more hands-on management style when there's a procrastinator in the group. If you find that a procrastinator is tripping up the flow of things in your office, you've got to ask yourself, "Who's in charge here; the procrastinator or me?"

Unlike the complainer, who is a nuisance more than a detriment to operations, the chronic procrastinator needs ongoing supervision. The good news is there are many things you can do to assist the procrastinator. You'll find an abundance of information about this topic in venues of all kinds. Do you have a child at home who procrastinates? When you seek information to help your child improve study habits, for example, you'll pick up tips to use with the workplace procrastinator, too. The more creative you are in handling this difficult employee the more likely you are to make headway.

PREDICTABLE PATTERN

The procrastinator wastes time thinking of excuses: "I can't do that!"

"It's time for an attitude adjustment," Laura comments to her assistant, Wendy. "We can meet Friday's deadline if we stop saying 'we can't' and start saying 'we *can* do this.'" Wendy thinks her boss has unrealistic expectations and doesn't believe for one minute that she can do the work by Friday. She puts the thick stack of numbers in the bottom desk drawer and types a letter. She responds to several interoffice e-mail messages and then works on the petty cash ledger. She makes a few entries before she pulls the stack of numbers out of the drawer again.

She doesn't see Laura enter the room, but Laura sees Wendy shaking her head when she looks at the numbers. "Let me help you get started," Laura suggests. "Begin with all the figures from the "A" states. Certainly you can tally Alabama, Alaska, Arizona, and Arkansas and input the information on the spreadsheet. That's all you'll do today, the four "A" states.

WHERE'S THE HARM?

a. Procrastinators have trouble starting a project. If this employee has good ideas to contribute you'll probably never hear about them. "I don't know where to begin, so how can I tell someone else about this? I won't mention it," she might think. This inability to focus on how to begin prevents her from mentioning her ideas.

Then, too, this sort of employee might simply procrastinate mentioning her idea, just like she procrastinates with everything else. As a result, this employee isn't a high performance type. Compared to her coworkers, the contribution she makes to the company's bottom line is minimal or satisfactory, at best.

b. Procrastinators are chameleons who might lead you down false pathways. A chronic procrastinator typically has a messy desk (although other excellent employees might have messy desks, too). "I don't have time for keeping my desk clean," claims the procrastinator. This employee's plan to tackle almost everything tomorrow impacts all that he or she does. You could send this employee to a time management seminar, or to work with an organizational consultant. You might even see signs of improvement after doing so. Still, you're only treating the symptoms, and you would probably achieve more by addressing the cause, if you can pinpoint it. (A list of possible causes appears at the end of this chapter.)

When Laura suggests that Wendy begin with the "A" states, she isn't concerned about Wendy's skills with the spreadsheet or her ability to understand the figures. She knows procrastinators have trouble getting started, and that's what she hones in on.

c. Procrastinators fear failure and hide perceived insufficiencies. Apparently, these employees are more afraid of failing at a task than they are of missing deadlines. "I'm only good at spreadsheet basics. I can't do the advanced stuff. I need time to figure things out," Wendy says to herself. She doesn't tell Laura. But, even if she had more self-confidence, she still doesn't know where to begin. She's dealing with a double whammy: weak organizational skills and fear of exposing her inadequate spreadsheet skills. Since procrastinators aren't forthcoming about fears, it takes x-ray vision for managers to be aware of them and the problems their reticence causes. Were she able to recognize Wendy's reservations, for example, Laura could instead assign this task to Jim, who is a whiz when it comes to manipulating spreadsheet software. Dealing with a procrastinator is like fighting your way out of a paper bag. The process can be exhausting, and sometimes you want to give up.

RECOMMENDATIONS

1. Partner the procrastinator with a coworker. This will usually take care of the getting-started component. The dynamics of a partnership, especially the shared responsibility, helps to cancel out concerns. Jim, for example, can demonstrate advanced spreadsheet techniques for Wendy. It's easier for a procrastinator to ask a partner for help than it is to confess to the boss she can't do something. A high-energy, pleasant coworker makes the best partner for a procrastinator. He or she brings a "cheerleader" quality to the venture. Most people work more effectively in a positive, pleasant environment and the procrastinator is no exception.

2. Ask the procrastinator to help with scheduling. Involvement enables this individual to make choices: "Let's do the difficult tasks first," or, "Let's start off easy and have little successes to point to before we tackle the tough assignments." Being in control boosts self-confidence.

These employees are also overwhelmed by a huge assignment. "We're going to entertain three executives from our Japan office. They'll be with us for five days and want a behind-the-scenes look at operations. You and Robinson will escort them. Show them everything." The words "Show them everything" reverberate in the procrastinator's head. Robinson, however, pulls out a pad and pen and asks, "What do you mean by everything?"

The boss replies, "The warehouse, our trucking facility, plant assembly lines, and our customer service department. After that, you can throw in the employee cafeteria and anything else that will help them get to know us better." Suddenly, "everything" has parts. It's manageable.

"One, enlist the aid of the warehouse supervisor to set up a tour. Two, meet with the customer-service chief to determine how best to introduce these operations to visitors. We're going to need to write out a schedule of events," contributes Robinson. Suddenly, the procrastinator sees "accomplishment" written all over this assignment. He visualizes handling some of the small assignments alone and successfully.

3. Let the good times roll. It's widely accepted that procrastinators' feelings are easily frayed. Many feel guilty, frightened, and doubtful of their abilities. Those who recognize that they're procrastinators aren't proud of this label. A manager who is good about celebrating small successes makes a difference. Remember Wendy? When she completes tallying Arizona, Arkansas, and Alabama and inputs the information on the spreadsheet, her manager, Laura, praises her achievement. "Couldn't have done better myself," she tells Wendy.

Words that praise are powerful rewards for a job well done, but don't stop there. A manager who has an arsenal of rewards to call upon won't have to work so hard to get the procrastinator to produce. "Plan to leave after lunch on Wednesday," Laura tells Wendy. "No need to be glued to your chair and your computer all week. We'll still meet the Friday deadline." This manager is putting her money where her mouth is, so to speak.

UNACCEPTABLE ATTITUDE

The procrastinator can't focus for any length of time: "I'll get back to this later. I need to check e-mail. I need to talk to the Office Manager. Oh, it's time for my break."

When a project manager procrastinates, unless the project has a life of its own—well, you can fill in the blanks. Ralph tells his boss, "I'm on it," when the company wins a contract to build ergonomic office furniture for a new client. His boss knows that nagging doesn't help, and when it looks as though Ralph is busy at his desk for long periods of time, his boss gives him the benefit of the doubt.

Ralph is a genius when it comes to design and is excited about the new business. Four days later, however, when the boss asks Ralph to show him the Gantt Chart, used to blueprint the sequence of events that leads to chair production, Ralph confesses. "I don't have it."

"Work on it for thirty minutes, and then come to see me," the boss replies. When thirty minutes have passed, Ralph arrives with a short list in-hand. He sweats profusely and is visibly strained. "Step into my office at ten and two each day and show me how the chart is developing," the boss instructs. Between those hours, the boss makes frequent stops at Ralph's desk to discuss the project. He offers tips and suggestions, and applauds many of Ralph's observations. Ralph follows this regimen for three days before he says, "I quit."

WHERE'S THE HARM?

a. Cross-training is out of the question when time is of the essence. Ralph may be a genius at design and excited about the new business, but he can't be expected to manage the project. He's not suited to this work. If the boss asks another employee to manage the project and that person struggles to do it, it's unlikely that he or she will quit. The procrastinator is operating on "overload" in this job and the strain has far reaching consequences. It's costly to hire and train employees, and the company takes a loss when they quit.

b. It takes extra time to coach the procrastinator. Ralph's coworkers do their jobs with far less input from the boss. Just think about all the other things the boss could be doing if he wasn't wasting so much time coaching this procrastinator. Time is money!

RECOMMENDATIONS

1. Stay involved and on top of these employees.
Use all the recommendations mentioned above: partner
the procrastinator with a coworker, ask this employee to
help with scheduling, praise and reward, and be on the
lookout for tips and suggestions all the time.

**2. Don't expect this employee to make a 180-
degree turnaround.** Applaud tiny changes and don't
expect more. The chronic procrastinator needs almost
constant oversight. One assumes this employee brings varied talents to the workplace and contributes to business
success. If not, this person probably should be dismissed.

In a Word . . .

Experts tell us workplace procrastination often occurs when employees:

1. Have insufficient information or skills to accomplish the task.

2. Are saddled with too much to do and too little time to do it.

3. Possess inadequate time management ability.

4. Are in poor physical condition and are either too weak or weary.

5. Have a fear of failure.

6. Dread being criticized.

7. Have a poor self-image.

8. Are not suited to the work, are not challenged, or are bored.

The chronic procrastinator has long-established patterns. Close friends assume this person won't be on time for dinner, the movies, or anything else. The reason for this behavior is probably unknown to the procrastinator and to you. Still, attempts to alleviate any one of the causes listed above are likely to meet with greater success than other measures. For example, you can send the procrastinator to numerous time management seminars, but if he has a problem getting started or a fear of failing he will continue to procrastinate. You need to get to the root of the true causes of procrastination if you want to rectify the problem.

THE KNOW-IT-ALL

HYPOTHETICALLY SPEAKING, if each company employee did know-it-all, business operations would always be in high gear and managers would always be smiling! In the real world, however, employees who really do know a lot often act self-importantly, impatiently, unconventionally, peculiarly, absent-mindedly, and standoffishly. Then there's the employee who just *thinks* he knows it all. This person isn't unusually intelligent, creative, quick, and capable like the others—but he'll never believe you if you tell him so.

People who act as though they know-it-all even though everyone else begs to differ have a high level of self-confidence. These employees probably won't ask for clarification or assistance, and they will bluff their way through assignments. It could take some time before the resulting errors are discovered.

PREDICTABLE PATTERN

A know-it-all exaggerates.

He or she embellishes, overstates, and—if you want to be blunt—outright lies. Consider the potential damage that could have occurred in a situation where Rosa, an employee who tends to be a know-it-all, misdirected a client. When her boss was away from the office and an important client called with a computer problem, Rosa, who was strolling near the boss's desk when the phone rang, answered it and assured him that she would handle it. "Mr. Carl, I'll have a messenger dispatched to your office with a new laptop computer before five." Mr. Carl told Rosa the damaged laptop would be boxed and waiting at the receptionist's desk.

"Oh, that's not necessary," Rosa responded. "You can just put it in the trash." Rosa seemed so sure of herself that the client didn't question her, even though he thought it strange that a laptop with a damaged keyboard was of no value. The more he thought about it, however, the more preposterous it seemed. Sure enough, Rosa had the new laptop at his office before five. He boxed the other laptop and put it on the floor of his office closet. Four weeks later, Rosa's boss was grateful that Mr. Carl still had the computer, especially since it retailed for $2,100. Rosa's company didn't want to *dump* this merchandise when the keyboard could easily be replaced. Fortunately, Mr. Carl graciously returned it to them.

In this situation, Rosa was puffed up with her own self-importance and proud of her quick action, which resulted in getting Mr. Carl a laptop replacement. But her unwarranted assuredness nearly came at quite a cost.

Where's the Harm?

a. These employees convince outsiders that they have more power, more control, or more of something else to offer than they do. That can prove to be disastrous. This time, Rosa's action benefited a client, but because she was flying by the seat of her pants, the positive outcome was a matter of luck. It was also a matter of luck that Rosa's company didn't have to forfeit the $2,100 computer. After all, Mr. Carl had no reason to believe that he couldn't keep it.

b. When you ask a know-it-all to evaluate something, you're likely to receive a stilted response. Heavy helpings of "I did this and I said that" are often sprinkled throughout his or her reply. Since you can't count on this employee to make unbiased assessments, the concepts of compromise and fairness are a hard sell! Both support workplace harmony. When harmony does prevail, the know-it-all practically guarantees that it won't last for long.

RECOMMENDATIONS

1. Point out the downside. Most employees want to succeed, and if they meet up with some bumps in the road, you come to the rescue with careful coaching and other time-tested management strategies. *As far as this employee is concerned, however, there aren't any bumps in the road he or she travels.* When you hear a know-it-all say something like, "I know what to do about this!" Be prepared to show him or her the bumps. Rosa's boss should address the situation immediately after becoming aware of what she had said: "Rosa, company policy forbids giving merchandise away free of charge without special permission. This includes damaged merchandise."

2. Work closely with this person. Even though you prefer to coach and cultivate employees, this individual can be an "accident waiting to happen" and not worth the risk. Your department's know-it-all may be a five on a scale of one to ten, with ten being a mega-know-it-all. You should never rely upon gossip and innuendo to make this determination, though—you'll take charge. If this person's behavior represents an acceptable risk, then he or she stays, but if his or her behavior causes too many problems, you'll have to plan a course of action.

UNACCEPTABLE ATTITUDE

A know-it-all thinks nothing of imposing or intruding.

Rosa didn't hesitate to answer the boss's telephone. She also didn't pause to ask another executive if she could hurry a replacement to Mr. Carl, even though she didn't know anything about this customer or the situation. Perhaps the first laptop computer was broken after Mr. Carl took possession of it.

WHERE'S THE HARM?

a. Rosa didn't have any background information and she didn't have the authority to act alone. It probably never occurred to her that she was overstepping her boundaries.

RECOMMENDATIONS

1. If you don't have the time or inclination to hover over this employee, assign her or him to work with one or two other people. But, be advised the know-it-all (who doesn't know-it-all) can frustrate coworkers. You'll want to check-in with that group often enough to recognize any signs of stress on the horizon. If the know-it-all is here to stay, you might have little choice but to hover.

2. Give this person praise when it's due. Your know-it-all employee might crave large helpings of praise. Rosa did act to assist a client. That's praiseworthy. If she's admonished about her methods without being praised for her deed, she's likely to be discouraged from acting to assist clients.

THE TRULY SMART KNOW-IT-ALL

Many times, when we think of an office know-it-all, a person like Rosa comes to mind. However, some people step into the workplace with an intellectual handle on their job requirements that is spectacular. Tech-savvy computer whizzes are a perfect example.

When you work with an unusually smart, creative, talented person, your attempts to control a situation are likely to be transparent. "Go ahead. Just try it," you can almost hear this sort of know-it-all thinking. "Who do you think you're dealing with, anyway?"

You might actually have to change the rules for this one person because doing so is a means to an end. You do know with whom you're dealing! Despite his or her impatience and sense of self-importance, all the positive things this know-it-all brings to the workplace make him a candidate for unique treatment. The know-it-all knows it, and you do, too.

Even though these individuals often get placed in the "difficult people" column they also belong in "the more the merrier" column. Let the competition beware of a company that employs large numbers of the brightest and best people in the field.

PREDICTABLE PATTERN

The know-it-all doesn't "see" boundaries.

Harry is an award-winning copywriter. His advertising campaigns produce dramatic sales increases for clients, and everyone associated with the agency refers to

Harry as the "boy genius." Not quite thirty, he's about the same age as Reggie, who manages the copywriting department.

Reggie never "pulls rank" on Harry, and all is well in the department until one morning when Harry walks into Reggie's office and says, "You've got to fire Joe Smith. I already told him he's going to be fired." He then turns abruptly and storms out.

Reggie doesn't miss a beat. He telephones Harry and says, "I don't tell you how to do your job and you shouldn't tell me how to do my job. If you think Joe Smith should be fired, come see me about it, and bring Joe with you."

Harry hangs up the telephone without saying a word.

WHERE'S THE HARM?

a. Know-it-all employees act impulsively, often more than other employees. Impulsive behavior comes with a predictable attachment: negative fallout. Presumably, Harry was upset with Joe Smith, and they had a confrontation. Joe might anticipate that Harry's threat has teeth. After all, Harry is the "boy genius," and others are likely to think that whatever this whiz kid says, goes. Potentially, Joe's fear of dismissal will cause him to be less productive. He might even take time off to look for another job. If the office gossips get wind of this incident, Reggie's credibility will be called into question, as coworkers wonder, "Who's the boss, anyway?"

b. Know-it-all employees arrive at conclusions fast. They process information quickly and are impatient to move on. This ability to "cut to the chase" is admirable, except at times when the action they take or recommend is a mistake. Pertinent information often slips through the cracks when the give-and-take process is shortened or omitted. Just because these types of know-it-alls know a lot about their chosen field, that doesn't mean they know *everything*. In the situation above, Reggie expects budget approval to hire another person with a new job title. He plans to offer the new position to Joe, whose skills are valuable but not well suited to his current job. Harry's arrogance and interference taint Reggie's plan. He can't act quickly without the staff thinking that Harry is pulling his strings. Moreover, thanks to Harry's outburst, Joe is likely to be suspicious about the new job offer.

RECOMMENDATIONS

1. Keep know-it-all employees well-informed about day-to-day operations. Management typically parcels out information to employees on a need-to-know basis. But these people sponge up information almost as naturally as they breathe. So why not give it to them? It might be the best way to make them aware of boundaries. Presumably, if Harry is aware that Joe Smith's weaknesses are recognized and change is planned, he'll have no reason to confront Smith. Beyond that, why not take advantage of a know-it-all's intelligence? These employees can contribute more if they know more about overall company goals and understand how daily operations are poised to achieve them. Plan to include these know-it-alls in at least 75 percent of your high-level business meetings, and see what happens. You can increase or decrease that percentage after you have a track record to evaluate.

2. Don't try to mold these people. Since managers manage, it's tempting to treat especially intelligent, creative, quick, and capable employees just like everyone else. In their case, however, less is more. The less you meddle and demand, the more you're likely to get from them. Their performance will be high and their allegiance will be strong. Remember Reggie? He didn't "pull rank" on Harry until one morning when Harry's action bordered on mutinous. When that happened, Reggie's quick action put an end to it.

UNACCEPTABLE ATTITUDE

The know-it-all has a peculiar approach to work style.

Shellie brings Starbucks coffee to the office each day in a clearly marked paper cup. She balances it on the right corner edge of her desk. Coworkers marvel that it doesn't fall over onto the pile of papers that never seems to diminish. Occasionally, she puts her head down on her desk and naps. She keeps several pairs of bedroom slippers in her office and doesn't wear shoes unless she leaves the building. When Shellie explains some things to her boss, he doesn't understand how her thought processes get from A to Z. They're both architects, and Shellie's approach to warehouse design is dazzling. The company they work for is a leader in their industry. Shellie works with two other architects who are very much like her. The boss just steps aside and lets them perform.

WHERE'S THE HARM?

a. Is there such a thing as too much freedom? A genius type employee is granted liberties that other employees are not granted. Does this undermine morale? When the boss doesn't understand an employee's explanation, is he or she acting recklessly by allowing the work to proceed anyway? The Shellies of this world are not cookie-cutter types. For many of them, a top performance is only possible when they have lots of room to do their work. The real question should be: Are you prepared to toss out the rulebook and benefit from what these people offer? Don't be too quick too answer. In the end, having a outlandish prima donna on staff can be especially taxing for managers and coworkers alike. If similar results can be obtained without these individuals, you might not want to hire them or keep them employed.

b. Weird behavior sends a message. If the mayor, banker, or potential new client arrives at the office and sees the chief architect asleep at her desk, what will come of it? If her slipper-wearing habit makes her the joke of the water cooler set, should you be concerned? If your genius lacks social graces, doesn't often communicate with coworkers, or calls attention to herself based upon other eccentricities, her being employed sends the message that the company endorses this behavior. People might sympathize with you and excuse weird behavior— if they accept this individual is wildly talented and nothing else counts. But they might also judge your company to be too strange or unconventional, and then choose to take their business elsewhere.

RECOMMENDATIONS

1. Don't put a peculiar employee on display. Spotlight this person's talents and achievements. There's no reason why the mayor or anyone else should see Shellie asleep at her desk. If you're thinking this puts you into the protection business, so be it. If your company genius has eccentricities that don't lend themselves to camouflage, don't tiptoe around the topic. "Sam, today we're setting up a photo display of the new campus buildings in the employee lounge. Two reporters will be here to interview you and Mike tomorrow. I know you like to wear your torn brown sweater and a Yankees baseball cap when you work. Please leave the sweater and cap behind when you come to the employee lounge. It's a matter of image building. We don't want to alienate any potential clients over an old sweater and a Yankees baseball cap."

2. Ask more questions, and insist on being kept in the loop. When you don't understand what the genius employee is attempting to explain, don't let your ego get in the way of asking questions. It might not be important for you to know mathematical formulae and technical details. Still, you should have a firm grasp of what's happening in your department. Ask questions until you get the answers you need. Remember, people process information in different ways. Maybe you need to see demonstrations or view visuals when words won't suffice. If all else fails, involve your supervisor or another colleague in the process. Or get it in writing. For example, ask the know-it-all to write a one-page progress report at defined intervals. Keep it short and simple. You don't want to distract this person from the main work, but you can't be left swinging in the breeze. If no one else in the company can assist you to check on progress, consider engaging an outside consultant. You don't want to risk confidentiality, but you might need some expert oversight so that you can sleep easier when day is done.

3. Show and insist upon mutual respect. Let these individuals know you admire their abilities and appreciate their contributions, but don't act self-deprecating. It's not okay if requests you make are ignored or responses seriously delayed. It's also not okay if policies and procedures others adhere to are completely disregarded. These employees can't just toss away the proverbial company rulebook. It's not easy to find a one-size-fits-all recommendation for giving and getting respect. The important thing is awareness. When you're working with know-it-all employees, don't lose your objectivity. Strive to maintain high professional standards for everyone.

In a Word . . .

There's a know-it-all who doesn't know much and a know-it-all who does. No matter which version you're managing, one thing is true: You can't do business as usual any longer. Initially, keep any know-it-all on a short leash! These folks can do damage quickly, but some can also propel the company forward to a new level of success. You, the manager, are likely to be the unsung hero or heroine when that happens. Sit a little taller in your chair and recognize that whichever style of know-it-all you live with, your best managerial talents will be put to the test.

THE SILENT TYPE

WHOEVER SAID "SILENCE IS GOLDEN" never worked with the silent type. This person makes you work harder to obtain the feedback that's part of everyday give-and-take with "normal" employees. When communication is limited to a few grunts, some headshakes, and an occasional complete sentence, the free and easy flow of ideas, observations, and concerns is essentially derailed.

Even when the silent type turns in a satisfactory job performance, a prudent manager takes steps to give this individual a platform from which to pontificate. It's best to do so sooner rather than later because without some way to vent, this individual is primed to erupt like a volcano eventually.

PREDICTABLE PATTERN

Negative criticism is problematic for the silent type.

Roger oversees sales for a new community of homes. He holds early morning staff meetings on Wednesday and Saturday mornings. Juan operates the back-office and is charged with generating sales reports people access electronically. He is considered a member of the sales team and attends staff meetings. Near the conclusion of each meeting, Roger asks if anyone has a question for Juan.

"I do," volunteers Rocky. "Is there some reason you don't highlight price changes? It's not easy to see them, and the other day I quoted an old figure to a customer. If he buys, I'll have to honor that price."

All eyes are on Juan, but before he can say anything, Sam speaks up. "Juan I asked you to include square-footage costs, and as of today, you haven't done it." When Mary adds something else, Juan all but melts into his chair. Later, he privately gives Roger explanations for all these things. He also says he doesn't want to attend staff meetings.

WHERE'S THE HARM?

a. Coworkers pull together to achieve goals. The silent type appears to pull away. When it's a matter of "them" and "us," it's unsettling when one of us doesn't identify with the rest of us. The silent type irritates the rest of the group because he or she is uncommunicative, and people fill in the empty spaces with their own interpretations. "Juan is lazy," or "Juan doesn't care," other members of the group might be incorrectly assuming. They focus on negatives because the silent type sends a message of rebuff: "I don't want to speak to you."

Juan, on the other hand, might be worried about a lisp or a stutter and might not want to speak. Perhaps he fears others will reject him because of these perceived frailties. There are many possible reasons for why Juan is a silent type, but none of them have to do with a desire to pull away from his coworkers purposely.

b. Communication is key to business success. When someone opts out of the circle, for whatever reason, that person works against business success. An old adage refers to a chain being as strong as its weakest link. Silent types weaken communication channels. In the highly competitive world in which your company conducts business, this doesn't bode well for success. If you have more than one silent type in your workplace, you have more than one weak link. In-your-face behavior and squeaky-wheel responses scream for attention, whereas silence doesn't. A well-informed manager hears the tree fall in the forest even when others don't. Consider silent types to be as potentially dangerous as falling trees!

RECOMMENDATIONS

1. Beef up communication channels. There's no need to single out silent types; instead, expose every member of your department to training or seminars that focus on improved communication. There are a variety of options you can draw on, including interactive computer courses, motivational speakers, and Toastmasters International meetings. Encourage employees to get up on their feet and speak to one another! It's an old-fashioned method for sharing information, but it's irreplaceable. Going away together in an outdoorsy setting, otherwise known as a retreat, is also a popular venue for some companies. Retreats accomplish myriad goals, and beefing up communication channels is tops among them.

2. Set an example. "Too elementary," you say? Before you make any assumptions, do some self-examination to evaluate how well you communicate verbally with your staff, colleagues, vendors, and customers. Keep it simple. Ask yourself what you want to get from communications during the course of a workday, and then ask yourself if you obtain the desired results. For example:

• Do I communicate clearly the first time I explain something, or do employees repeatedly question me after I give instructions?

• Do employees meet deadlines? If not, should I break down requests into more manageable parts? Or, is there another reason deadlines aren't met?

• Am I a good listener, or do I simply deliver soliloquies? (Communication involves more than one person—a speaker and a listener—and the two must switch off for the conversation to be effective.)

• Do I approach everything as though I'm a know-it-all? (People don't respond well to know-it-all types.)

UNACCEPTABLE ATTITUDE

The silent type is a loner and zones out when it comes to company news.

Trudy eats lunch alone. She props up a book in front of her place at the cafeteria table and coworkers don't intrude. The book serves as a barrier and Trudy knows it. The Human Resource Director recently advised employees of benefits changes and possible choices. For almost a week, employees discussed the topic as they ate lunch. Trudy, however, tuned it all out, so she was unaware of nuances related to the dental benefits program. And although she knew that her boss was getting married soon, Trudy wasn't aware that she was taking a three-week honeymoon. She hadn't even read the bulletin board postings that announced the dates that the office corridors would be painted.

When the time came, Trudy didn't select the proper dental benefits to suit her needs. And after her boss left to get married, Trudy incorrectly informed callers that her boss would return at the end of the week. She even leaned on a freshly painted wall one day and got wet paint all over her new jacket.

WHERE'S THE HARM?

a. The silent type is insulated and frequently ostracized. Whether or not she intends to do so, this person sends out a negative vibe that implies "I'm better than you are" to others around her. As a result, she falls out of favor with coworkers and that's not a good place to be. Plenty of useful information is frequently exchanged through the company grapevine. But the silent type doesn't "get it," and she can't utilize this method to spread information.

Maybe Trudy speaks Spanish fluently and is a speedy, accurate translator. Or maybe she could really use some overtime pay and would be willing to work weekends. What if she needs to carpool with somebody for the next few weeks, because her car is getting fixed? Trudy could benefit by putting this information out to people, so it can circulate through the grapevine. Her Spanish speaking skills could lead to a new and well-paid position. Or she might be asked to work weekends and earn extra money. She could even discover people who are already carpooling and have room for one more.

The silent type works at a disadvantage because she operates as an "outsider" without benefit of this kind of privileged information. This lack of information doesn't just affect her; it affects her boss and her customers, too.

b. Loners aren't picked for the team. Team-effort is an integral part of the office environment. Working together to meet a deadline or to win a prize (for being the department with the greatest safety record, for instance), or to support a coworker (raising money to help an employee and his family after a fire destroys their home) is standard operating procedure in workplaces throughout the country. But the standoffish silent type won't be asked to participate unless it's unavoidable, because he or she dampens down everyone's enthusiasm for achievement.

"Sally doesn't care if she's late for work. We can't win an on-time-all-month award with her in our group. We're sunk before we begin," the colleagues of a silent type might say. Even if Sally is willing to put in the effort and go the extra mile to achieve any goal, her coworkers expect the worst from her, simply because they never know where she stands with things—or where they stand with her. Battles are sometimes lost before they begin owing to group expectations.

RECOMMENDATIONS

1. Arrange for an audition. If you're a boss trying to draw a silent type out of his shell, try asking this employee questions that can't be answered with a simple response. Listen carefully, and ask follow up questions. In your one-on-one conversation, give this individual the opportunity to explore a subject thoroughly. Make note of valuable observations. Then, the next time a small gathering of employees assembles, credit the silent type for those insights. Or, if he didn't say anything especially worthy of note, ask him a related question at this point. Suddenly, the silent type will be responding to an issue he's already thought about because of your earlier conversation with him. At this point, he knows he has something of value to contribute. Repeat the process you used earlier. Ask questions that can't be answered with a simple "yes" or "no." Turn this one-on-one audition opportunity into a regular "happening." It could be that this person will begin to participate without prodding once he or she realizes, "I can do this!"

2. Open your door. When most employees want to speak to you and your door is closed, they just usually return at another time. But the silent type might find this too difficult. Make this person feel welcome almost any time. Let it be known to all that you're approachable. "How will I get my work done?" you ask. Remember, this is also part of your work. People will eventually grow accustomed to your open door and most aren't likely to take advantage of it. When someone enters unannounced make him feel welcome and work to assist him to get to the point quickly. Then, you can both return to work.

If a constant open-door invitation isn't practical, open your door every morning or every afternoon. If the silent type still never approaches you, invite him to do so. "Carl my door is open every morning and I hope you'll step in to chat sometime." Don't contrive words—be straightforward. And, don't let anyone leave your office without thanking him or her for the information provided. On the chance that an employee wears out his welcome, ask him to jot down concerns and keep his visits to no more than twice a week.

3. Give this person fifteen minutes of fame. When possible, permit this individual's professional skills to be spotlighted. For example, Veronica was an excellent graphics artist who almost never spoke. Her boss decided to use her talents "in house," and asked her to make posters to remind employees to keep the lunchroom clean, to wear nonskid shoes when working in the warehouse, and to wash hands before they exited the men's and women's rooms. She designed an especially humorous graphic for reminding people to wash their hands. In fact, it was so good that her boss asked the editor of the employee newsletter to feature it in an article. He took every opportunity to make Veronica a star among her peers.

Playing up Veronica's achievement gave her colleagues something positive to approach her about, and that helped to break the ice. In time, people just naturally approached her and pulled her along with them. They'd ask her to have lunch at their table and be a part of group projects. The success of this strategy is highly dependent upon the good nature of fellow employees and the manager's creativity. Veronica's "talent" is easy to spotlight. Focus on a person's professional or creative skills, and you're likely to find something to crow about!

In a Word . . .

Do everything possible to help the silent type improve communication skills. Free-flowing and productive communication nourishes success in your department and in the company. Yet, it's all too easy to ignore an employee who isn't exactly "in your face." Use skillful coaching methods to help this person become a contributor. The good news is, the "silent type" can change. Progress can be quick and steady. As a matter of fact, this person could become one of the most adept communicators on your staff. Put on your mentoring hat and make it happen!

THE SOCIAL BUTTERFLY

SOMEONE WHO FINDS IT EASY to chat and interact with virtually everyone is usually a delightful person to have as an employee. This individual probably excels at providing customer service and might assist the "silent type" employee, and others like "the rookie" or "overly sensitive" employees, to integrate with the rest of the group. The only time the social butterfly is likely to make a blip on the "negaholic" radar is when tasks are not being tackled or completed, or when there's a lapse in professional demeanor.

When the social butterfly isn't staying on top of assignments, people on the receiving end of this person's sociability are distracted from their work, too. Productivity takes an all-around nosedive. Multiply what might seem like a negligible productivity loss by fifty weeks a year, and it's not a small matter.

PREDICTABLE PATTERN

Social butterflies ask lots of questions.

Maria maintains company records for twenty truckers. She can tell you a good deal about the drivers because she chats at length with all of them. When Bob's daughter had her tonsils removed, Maria sent her a card. She checked with Bob frequently until she heard the little girl had returned to school. When Stella was preparing to fly to Denver to attend her sister's wedding, Maria brought her a magazine article that explained all about Denver and the airlines that service it. Maria checked with Stella often about the upcoming trip. "Do you have your dress? Will you take some extra time off so you can do some sightseeing in Denver while you're there?"

Many of Maria's coworkers appreciate her interest in them and the thoughtful little things that she does. These drivers must clock out their trucks and they do that promptly, but when they return at the end of their shifts, they hang out in Maria's office. Lately, Maria's statistical input runs twenty-four hours late. One day, her boss mentions that he inadvertently gave the Union Representative day-old figures. "I'm in hot water with this Union guy because I assumed you keep records up-to-the-minute," he told her.

After that, Maria rushed to input information in a timely manner, but she made mistakes. "What's going on Maria? We placed orders based on your statistics and then find out, the figures you gave us are wrong," her boss asked. "Now it's not just a Union guy getting angry. This time we ordered supplies we didn't even need yet."

Where's the Harm?

a. The social butterfly isn't 100 percent reliable. A capable employee who has a long track record as a social butterfly gets to a place where he or she is "spread too thin." At that point, delays and errors are inevitable.

b. Some people question motives. The extreme neighborly attentions the social butterfly exhibits are not always welcome in the workplace. Some people are suspicious about this person's intentions. Bill's wife was upset when their little girl received a get-well card from Maria. "Why does this woman know about our daughter?" she asked her husband.

"We're just friendly," he responded.

"Don't be naïve, Bill. She could be a troublemaker," observed his wife.

Managers can't concern themselves about what some people choose to think. Still, workplace behavior that's extreme can set the stage for unpleasant repercussions.

c. The social butterfly might know too much. When a person tells someone else more than she or he should, that person often regrets it. For example, "I'm exhausted. My husband was out drinking with his pals until the wee hours last night. I couldn't sleep because I was so worried. And then I had to go out, pick them all up, and drive them to their homes. Men!" This confessor might later be embarrassed about revealing sensitive information and do something nasty to discredit the social butterfly who is all too eager to lend an ear. The person who manages these two will get stuck dealing with the dissention that results. Even though the Social Butterfly isn't directly responsible for this state of affairs, the intimate climate he or she creates acts like a magnet for such occurrences.

RECOMMENDATIONS

1. Put the social butterfly to work where this ability is an unqualified asset. Social butterflies are not always identified when they're interviewed for a position. It's obvious that Maria's talents, for example, are wasted in a job that is best done by a person who can work for long periods with records and statistics without much human interaction. It might not be possible to reposition your social butterfly right away. While you're waiting for a more suitable position to become available, why not shift some responsibilities to the social butterfly? For example, are there predictable periods when customers or clients call your offices with orders or complaints? If your business is impacted by the seasons (e.g., you sell clothing to skiers or manufacture scoreboards for college football games) or major holidays, the telephones are busier with incoming calls and e-mail volume increases at those times. Instead of hiring the usual part-timers or seasonal workers for these tasks, let your social butterfly do the job. Then engage the part-timers to do some of the work the social butterfly normally handles.

2. Counsel the social butterfly. Let this person know that although you admire his or her social skills, these tendencies must be reigned-in at work. "You're an excellent people person. I wonder if you would like a position where you can use these skills to help the company? It's not possible to make the most of your skills with coworkers because each of us has a job to do and too much time spent chatting and showing concern for others distracts people from doing their work." Accentuate the positive and your social butterfly might tuck in his or her wings and cooperate with you.

You might also give this employee the responsibility of planning office parties, or encourage her to use her people skills in the community. For instance, you could ask this employee if she might like to represent the company in a Literacy Volunteers program, or some other charitable cause.

UNACCEPTABLE ATTITUDE

This person is literally a hands-on individual!

Although hugs and similar intimacies are unacceptable in the workplace, they're standard operating procedure for the social butterfly. He or she thinks nothing of stroking someone's arm, or giving someone a hug or even a backrub. It's rare that you encounter the social butterfly without receiving or witnessing the passing of a hands-on message. The problem is, these messages can be misunderstood. They might also be considered sexual harassment. Even if you believe the social butterfly is innocent of such intentions, others may differ. When a male employee, for example, flutters around from one female employee to the next, taking his chitchat and his touchy-feely ways with him, accusations of improper conduct are sure to follow.

WHERE'S THE HARM?

a. When suspicions of sexual harassment are raised, workplace harmony will cease and desist. That's bad for employees. That's bad for business. A lawsuit could result, which can be both costly and embarrassing for your company. Even if the court decides in favor of the defendant, the publicity can still be bad for business and do your company considerable harm.

b. These unacceptable displays of behavior announce that everyday business etiquette takes a backseat in your department. When that happens, competency is called into question.

Let's say a manufacturer's representative pays calls to dozens of medical offices. She trains people on the use of diagnostic machinery and monitors their efficiency.

Most employees are proficient and serious about proper use of the equipment her company leases to doctors. Six times a year, she stops to see the office manager of a medical office near the edge of town. Each time she drives away from the meeting she realizes how different this office is from the others. The office manager is a social butterfly and instead of shaking her hand and conducting himself in a business-like manner, he is overly friendly and lacks discretion.

The representative notices safety issues don't receive the attention they do at the other offices. She asks her boss to accompany her on one of these visits. She says nothing that hints at the customer's lack of professionalism. As soon as they leave the premises, her boss says, "This man is in the wrong business. You would expect a little more decorum from the office manager of a medical office." Later, her boss tells her to take this client off of her visiting schedule. "We're removing our diagnostic machinery from that office the first chance we get." She never learns more but suspects that her company isn't willing to sanction the use of their equipment in an office where sound practices are questionable.

Recommendations

1. Talk to your staff about ethics, diplomacy, courtesy, and professionalism. The social butterfly's attitudes and behaviors aren't associated with serious business. When you have one or more employees who fit this description, you need to spend time talking about ethics, diplomacy, courtesy, and professionalism. Schedule an informal lunch meeting where the company provides lunch, and lead the talk yourself or invite an outside speaker (a lawyer or business graduate school professor, for instance) to attend the gathering. If your company has a Human Resources department, you can ask for help to set up training sessions. Remind employees that behavior that's too relaxed or overly familiar can work to send the wrong message to customers and clients. This must be an on-going effort, and all personality types should be included in these information seminars and activities, not just the Social Butterflies.

2. Ask the social butterfly to solve people problems. Since this individual is a natural people person, invite him or her to brainstorm with you and others on issues such as:

- Absenteeism

- Tardiness

- High turnover

Don't be surprised if these aspiring management gurus pinpoint some new reasons that haven't yet occurred to you, such as higher absenteeism during hunting season, flu season, and so on. Social butterflies can alert you to all sorts of other factors as well. Perhaps several of your employees have been tardy lately because their new babies have been keeping them up all night. Maybe others are missing work because a new shopping mall recently opened in town, and their spouses, who had previously been stay-at-home parents, are suddenly out working, so someone needs to take care of the kids. You might even find out that you're losing people to your competitor, who offers employees perquisites, like opportunities to win trips and other prizes, unlike your own company.

Social butterflies are privy to news they hear through the grapevine, and they process that news differently. Toss questions out to them about how to make things better. Be willing to try unconventional remedies. In addition to solving problems, you might generate some good publicity. Just imagine the headlines: "Local company sends new parents to a hotel to get some sleep." Or, "A nurse is hired to work the nightshift at home."

3. Tap into the persuasiveness reservoir. Social butterflies are persuasive individuals. That's not surprising since they listen carefully and respond to a person's needs. This is an important skill for a salesperson to cultivate, and there are times when each of us, regardless of chosen profession, is a salesperson.

Jake was in charge of late-afternoon operations at the Mill. He was convinced he could reduce absenteeism if employees would wash their hands more often during this shift. All his efforts to "sell" cleanliness were of limited value until Midge, the resident social butterfly, got interested. "I don't get it, Midge. We have new soap dispensers, softer paper towels, and four new clean-up stations so no one has to walk very far to wash their hands. These are good health measures. It's simple, but no one is paying attention." Midge asked Jake lots of questions, like "How do you know that clean hands result in less time lost?" and "How much did it cost to install new clean-up stations?"

About one week later, Jake noticed an increase in hand washing. He questioned Midge. "I told folks when they wash more often they don't bring so many germs home to their wives and kids. I mentioned that study you told me about, and I explained how much the company spent to make it easy for us to wash our hands."

Social butterflies persuade people by honing in on benefits. Although employees weren't motivated by Jake's "Wash hands, reduce absenteeism" crusade, their ears perked up when they heard Midge's message about not bringing so many germs home, and they responded accordingly. "The company spent $25,000 to upgrade our facilities. They don't get much in return but we do," people responded.

In a Word . . .

Business is serious stuff and social butterfly types tend to trivialize it. They might never do so intentionally, but that does not matter. Focus on harnessing the people-to-people talents that come so naturally to these individuals. As a matter of fact, you might be able to learn social butterfly "graces" from this employee. It's flattering to this individual when you emulate her approach. Just don't be lulled into a comfort-zone when things are going well, because the social butterfly usually can't distinguish between friendly, caring behavior and behavior that oversteps "business boundaries." It's probably a waste of time to expect otherwise, so remain vigilant.

THE "NO PEOPLE SKILLS" PERSON

THE PHRASE FOOT-IN-THE-MOUTH was probably invented after observing the "no people skills" employee in action. This person might be highly skilled at all other aspects of the job, but when it comes to interaction with coworkers, customers, or management, this person is way off the mark.

He's not just honest, he's blunt. When he's sincere, he's gushy. If she's complimentary, it sounds phony. When she's in a hurry, she's abrupt. It's not surprising that the "no people skills" employee is something of a pariah.

Human Resource personnel can learn to recognize and avoid hiring this sort. It's arguably easier to teach a "people person" how to accomplish job tasks than it is to teach a "no people skills" person how to become a "people person." Don't despair, however, if you already have one or more of these individuals in your midst. Some experts claim these employees can learn to smooth out their rough edges. Someone will have to initiate changes, however, and that someone is probably going to be you, the manager.

Predictable Pattern

The one thing that's predictable is that this "negaholic" is unpredictable!

The "no people skills" employee might be afraid of making mistakes and worried that people will laugh at her. Or, this employee might not care about what others think of her. Or, strange as it seems, this employee might be capable of feeling both ways—albeit not at the same time.

Donna acted obnoxiously during a staff meeting, but afterward her boss found her teary eyed in the hallway. Donna claimed she was nervous and when she gets nervous she says things she doesn't mean. Donna's boss had another meeting to attend and hurried along but she thought about the hallway encounter. About one week later, she came upon Donna shouting at a parts delivery-man. Based upon past incidents, she assumed Donna didn't care what other people thought, but then she remembered the hallway confession. Was something currently making Donna nervous?

If you're alert to the unpredictable nature of this type of employee, you won't put yourself on automatic pilot! The boss sent an e-mail to Donna: "Is there a problem with the parts delivery? Please explain." She was determined not to act until she learned more from Donna. Donna responded, "I was asked to sign for boxes that weren't delivered. This man is a cheat." Even though Donna's people skills aren't always the greatest, this time there was provocation and reason for her loudly delivered indignation. The boss instructed Donna on how to report vendor complaints. Other measures were unnecessary.

WHERE'S THE HARM?

a.   Managers fall prey to disappointments and deploy knee jerk responses. It's never business as usual when you're dealing with "negaholics." Remember, you're only human and will feel taxed by these individuals if you don't watch out!

b.   Calm periods are not necessarily followed by more of the same. The "no people skills" person might perform satisfactorily for a time and then revert to old habits. Sid slams the telephone down when a vendor says he can't make the delivery in the afternoon. Margaret tells the customer if she doesn't want the dress in the color blue she had better shop elsewhere. Paul tells Chuck, his coworker, he looks fat after Chuck mentions that he lost weight. These types can be so unpredictable that you might as well check the night sky to see if there's a full moon whenever they revert to their nasty ways. Yours is not to reason why! Yours is to be prepared for twists and turns as you attempt to guide this individual to display acceptable people skills more consistently.

RECOMMENDATIONS

1. When someone displays poor to intolerable people skills, others consider the display a personal affront. You shouldn't take it personally, and neither should your other employees.

2. Plan the work and work the plan might be applicable advice most days for achieving most goals. The "no people skills" employee strains that strategy. A "plan" might work well until one day when it doesn't work at all. Unless your original "plan" includes switching quickly to another "plan," you'll be stymied.

UNACCEPTABLE ATTITUDE

"No people skills" types have no qualms about being rude.

When the ABZ Bakery was automated all jobs were redesigned. Frank, who previously worked alone, was assigned to work with five coworkers in the packaging room. "Each person will be cross-trained so that any one person can take over for another," announced the Human Resource manager. Frank twisted around in his seat and didn't look at her. He kept thumping his foot up and down as she spoke and he clicked the back of a pencil on the table in front of him. After she distributed some written instructions, she wished everyone well and left the building.

The packaging team huddled together. "Come on, Frank, join us," Norman called. Norman bent over backwards to please everyone.

Frank sauntered over and sat down but left soon after he said, "She must know you're a bunch of dummies."

The next day, Norman asked Frank, "How are you today, Buddy?"

Frank jumped back as Norman extended his hand for a handshake. "I'm going out for a smoke," he said. "All this lovely work-together stuff makes me want to puke."

WHERE'S THE HARM?

a. Time is wasted. Team members should concentrate on their jobs. Instead, they focus on drumming up cooperation from a rude individual. As hours and weeks pass and their efforts are unsuccessful, they will devise methods for excluding or avoiding this individual. In either case, employees are not free to work at the tasks for which they earn their salaries. Instead of moving from point A to point B, people must detour along the route to "handle" this difficult worker.

b. This individual doesn't empathize with others or worry about consequences. When Frank said aloud, "She must know you're a bunch of dummies," he stepped over the line. If the Human Resource manager said nothing to make anyone feel less empowered, valuable, or respected, it appears that only Frank came away with this impression. Moreover, his phrasing left no doubt in interpretation, since he conveniently left himself out of the statement. Why did he make such a reckless remark? Didn't he know it would make people feel badly? Didn't he care? The "no people skills" employee doesn't think about repercussions.

c. The company gets blamed when "outsiders" are offended. If this individual lets off steam at the drop of a hat, it's conceivable that a customer, client, or vendor will be on the receiving end of thoughtless statements. It's one thing to keep it all-in-the-family—coworkers might know that Frank, for example, is an expert cake decorator, and so they witness his "up" side. However, others outside the company only know of his ugly behavior. They question how this company can employ such a person. Some people will be quick to blame the company for the shabby treatment they receive from the "no people skills" employee. "I won't buy anything from the ABZ Bakery! Those people are awful," customers might decide. This guilt-by-association phenomenon is not a rarity.

RECOMMENDATIONS

1. Prepare personnel charged with hiring to recognize the individual who fits this description. One method for detecting the "no people skills" job candidate is via personality testing. (The Myers-Briggs Personality Test is a popular aid. Browse the Internet for more information or to locate other tests.) Even without a written test, this person is likely to reveal him or herself during an interview. It's essential that company-hiring personnel be well trained to listen. People are predictably nervous during a job interview and might unwittingly tap a foot or a pencil on a desk, but if the interviewer is paying careful attention to responses, it should be easy to detect serious "no people skills" behavior. If you elect to hire a "no people skills" person because she brings other attributes to the company, at least you're forewarned about what to expect.

2. Pour on the employee training! Send employees to "people skills" seminars or subscribe to newsletters that emphasize courteous behavior in the workplace. Everyone can use a refresher, so there's no need to single out the "no people skills" employee for seminar attendance. Send everyone.

Don't settle for broad-brush programs. Look for specifics. Will attendees discover how body language impacts communication? How about improved listening skills—will those be discussed and will the right and wrong way to listen be demonstrated?

Use all possible resources to keep this topic front and center. Hang posters in the lunchroom or employee lounge that inspire "people skills." (For example: "Since you have one mouth and two ears, please try listening more and talking less," or "Give your smiles away.") Books and short films that spotlight people skills are available, too. Lend them to employees who might want to read or view them at home. Or, designate some time each month to view and discuss these films and books.

Sharpening your own people skills is also a work-in-progress, so no matter how adept you are in this arena, take steps to get better and better. When you set a fine example, the "no people skills" employee can't help but notice.

3. Explain why. These employee might not realize that weak people skills detract from performance and derail personal success. Before you invite this person in to talk, make some notes. Jot down recent incidents that to help demonstrate the point. "When Jen won the employee of the month parking space, most of us congratulated her." Discuss why people enjoy recognition. Talk about how a winner might respond if coworkers ignore the achievement.

You don't need a script, but think before you speak. Avoid discussing the employee's actions (for instance, "I noticed you left the room and didn't say anything to Jen"). You don't want this individual to become defensive. You want to demonstrate that people do business with people they like. "In effect, we do business with coworkers all the time. Saying congratulations is a nice thing to do." Keep it simple. Keep it brief. This individual probably has a short attention span when discussing people skills. (Be sure to read Chapter 16: The Last Resort: Disciplinary Action and Termination. It discusses responsibilities you have, under the law, and alerts you to actions that are designed to protect you and the company.)

UNAPPROACHABLE ATTITUDE

Virtually everyone likes to be liked but this person may not show it.

Most of the negative employees you've read about so far demonstrate a variety of *unacceptable* attitudes. The "no people skills" person doesn't exactly have an *unacceptable* attitude in this instance, but his or her inapproachability is a problem, nevertheless.

Praise is as important to the "no people skills" employee as it is to every other employee. It just might be difficult for you to want to give praise to someone who has no people skills. Because these types aren't warm or approachable, it might feel like the praise is a one-way street. As a manager, however, it's your job to rise above that. Since this employee is often skilled at his or her work, focus on the work and let this person know you appreciate a job well done. "José, the visual aids you added to the Warehouse Inventory Report are excellent. The bar graph makes it especially easy to tell how quickly stock is rotated."

WHERE'S THE HARM?

a. Even the most congenial people you know often find it awkward to accept a compliment. "You like my dress? This old thing?" The "no people skills" employee is likely to have an even harder time with compliments, and there's a greater chance that he might respond inappropriately. Most people would say "thank you" or, smile. This employee might ignore your comment, minimize it, or say something that's insulting, such as, "You should have recognized the importance of visual aids a long time ago."

RECOMMENDATIONS

1. Be judicious with accolades if this employee may eventually be dismissed. Even when you only say what you mean and don't embellish your praise of this employee with anything but the facts, praise can be used against you. Unless you're careful, this person might be left thinking: "He always praises my work, so he must have fired me because he doesn't like me, or because I earn too much money, or because I'm fat," or for any number of illegal reasons.

2. Use off-the-record employee performance reviews as needed. Typically, both employer and employee contribute input to the EPR. Conduct the periodic EPR as usual, but from time to time pull it out of the file to peruse on your own. It should assist you to keep things in perspective.

In a Word . . .

People like to "do business" with people they like. A "no people skills" employee hasn't got what it takes to charm anyone. This individual is likely to be ostracized and, therefore, be about as effective as a hermit. If this employee's lack of savoir-faire escalates to the point of rudeness, the company will suffer the consequences. The disdain the company earns might even be well deserved. Conscientious managers won't permit rude individuals to represent the company. People who work for the company deserve courteous treatment, too. If you can't assist the "no people skills" person to reform with dispatch, give it up or hide him. If it's not practical or possible for the "no people skills" employee to work alone, you have little choice but to plan for his or her dismissal.

THE ROOKIE

A ROOKIE IS ANYONE who has been recently hired. Some of these individuals are fresh out of school and have little or no work experience. Others have work experience but might be unfamiliar with your industry. These employees aren't particularly difficult in the "negaholic" sense that the previous personality types were. Presumably, however, all rookies are new to your company, and each one needs guidance and coaching. That's the only reason why the rookie is included in this section of *Managing Difficult People*. When a rookie arrives on the scene, expect to carve out a segment of time to assist that individual with "getting up to speed," or designate another employee to do so. Or, do both.

Eleanor Smith joined the firm just days after graduating from college. Helen Jones left the teaching profession to join the marketing department of the same firm. Each was a rookie. Jones had work experience. Smith did not. Smith had a degree in accounting and was hired as an accountant. Jones was hired because she was smart and eager to participate in a marketing training program. She had two undergraduate degrees: one in education and the other in marketing.

Who would remain a rookie longer—Smith or Jones?

You might be inclined to answer, Smith. After all she's completely new to the workplace and probably has less life-experience because she's younger than Jones. In reality, it's practically impossible to predict with accuracy which one will be a rookie longer. Some executives consider any rookie's tenure to be five years long. Others claim it's TIS (the industry, stupid). Rookie computer programmers, for example, "get up to speed" quickly, whereas the learning curve for rookie sales personnel is lengthy.

On the plus side of the equation, rookies with little work experience are generally eager to learn and eager to please management. They don't have bad habits to unlearn. And, they earn at the low end of the salary rainbow. The downside of this equation is that they need to be nurtured and sometimes pampered. Rookies need praising and mentoring. They require considerable tender love and care, and someone—or more than "one"—has got to do it. Rookies can drain your energies and resources.

PREDICTABLE PATTERN

Rookies don't don camouflage.

Rookies are eager to please. Ah, but what does it take to please? A rookie doesn't know. During the early period of employment when this individual is getting the "lay of the land" he or she is clueless and, therefore, what you see is what you get. This might never happen again!

WHERE'S THE HARM?

a. This condition actually works in management's favor. Remember the only reason the rookie is discussed in this section of the book is because he or she will require considerable time and attention.

Now is the time to get to know the "person" inside of the employee. Is he or she a stickler for details, does he hate to be late, does she take direction well, are they both easily overwhelmed?

b. Protect the company's investment. The rookie is vulnerable and you don't want to lose him after you invest time and money to find, hire, and train him. The rookie won't readily identify the difficult coworkers in the workplace. If you have a "no people skills" employee routinely interacting with a rookie, the rookie might fade under that pressure. Don't put the rookie to the test.

c. You might expect more from the rookie than you should expect. Give the rookie room to grow and provide opportunities so the rookie can stretch and discover, "I can do it!"

But tread lightly. One excellent achievement does not a seasoned employee make. If a major client needs special attention, don't send the rookie to do the job alone. The key word here is: alone. And, it might be you shouldn't involve the rookie in anything that pertains to a major client. Since rookies don't typically don camouflage, they probably can't display the finesse a more seasoned employee would bring to the assignment. "Mr. Carter, we can't do that," has a different ring to it than "Mr. Carter, I'll put that request in to our warehouse manager immediately. I'll get back to you within the hour."

RECOMMENDATIONS

1. Identify more than one employee who can help to train the rookie. The rookie will learn better from at least two different personalities and from exposure to two different work styles. This way, the rookie won't get "married" to one approach, which he or she is prone to do at this early stage. (Remember, a rookie is eager to please.) Tom was a "detail man," and when Andrew, a rookie, worked with Tom, he got into the habit of checking every detail. Francine had the ability to multitask and didn't give details her immediate attention. She kept a daily log and updated the log just before leaving the office each day. As she retraced her steps in her memory, she took care of or noted details that would need attention. Andrew probably wasn't aware of it at the time, but he discovered that he could favor his own preferences when he was in charge. For example, Andrew didn't enjoy morning meetings because he was energy charged and wanted to act, not plan. After lunch, he found he was far more productive at meetings. This unspoken lesson has the potential of favorably impacting his entire work career.

2. Give the rookie feedback. Almost everyone thrives on praise, but the rookie is in unfamiliar territory and is truly dependent on feedback. When a rookie asks, "How am I doing?" whether it's praise or constructive criticism, deliver it. Don't make the rookie guess what you're thinking about his or her performance—speak up! Make it a point to do so two or three times a week, or as often as you think appropriate. It's a little like drinking eight glasses of water a day: You might have good intentions, but you probably won't do it unless you consciously make it happen!

Since the rookie is vulnerable, it's probably good to deliver the good news first: "Christina, you handled that complaint well. But, here's a tip that can practically guarantee a positive outcome each time you reply to an unhappy customer." In this case, you would advise Christina to listen carefully to the customer, and when she responds, use some of the words the customer used. (This is borrowed from a communication strategy known as mirroring.)

For example, if Mr. Alfonso says, "This is no way to treat a customer. The serviceman said he had to order the parts. Why don't you keep the parts on-hand?"

Then, the rookie might respond, "Mr. Alfonso, we normally keep the parts on-hand. The serviceman must have been surprised to find he had to order the parts. If we can't repair the copier by tomorrow, we'll lend you another copier." The phrases "parts on-hand" and "order the parts" are familiar to Mr. Alfonso—they're his words. If you use them, too, this shows him that you must be aligned with him. Is this why mirroring works? Theoretically speaking, yes. (Test it yourself and evaluate the outcome.)

Of course, you'll introduce your own tips to a rookie. Sometimes, your feedback won't be pretty. Just say it and move on. "Customers expect us to be available from 8:00 A.M. until 6:00 P.M. No excuses. You jeopardize your job when you're not punctual. If you want to talk about this, my door is open. Otherwise, I'll expect to see you at your desk at 8:00 A.M. sharp."

UNAVOIDABLE OUTCOME

Rookies may make more mistakes than seasoned employees.

This is one area where the rookie really differs from other employee types. When you expect mistakes you'll install fail-safe measures and minimize nasty spills. You don't want to make a rookie feel as though he is walking on a tight rope, but you will want to monitor some assignments closely. One way to do this is to ask for feedback at frequent, well-defined, intervals. As time moves on and the rookie knows more about the job, ask for feedback less often. A set of training wheels serves a useful purpose on a child's bicycle. Eventually the child builds confidence and asks for them to be removed. Corny as it might be, you are the rookie's training wheels!

WHERE'S THE HARM?

a. The training-wheel stage might last too long. If the rookie doesn't demonstrate she's ready to ride without them within a reasonable period of time, you'll want to intervene. Pep talks and coaching come to your aid. "You input all the numbers perfectly on the last monthly reports. There's nothing unusual about this month's activity. You can do it! I don't need to see it. When it's ready, send it directly to the chief financial officer."

b. Know the difference between "good mistakes" and "bad mistakes" (for example, revealing confidential information is a bad mistake). Just because you're prepared for the rookie to make more mistakes than other employees doesn't mean that all mistakes are acceptable. Serious mistakes, especially those that are repeated, suggest you've hired the wrong person for the job. The rookie might have exaggerated his skills and experience when he was interviewed. Or, he's not suited to the work and without a crystal ball no one could have known. Should the rookie be transferred to another department? Should the rookie be enrolled in a skills-teaching class? Take necessary action so that serious mistakes aren't repeated.

RECOMMENDATIONS

1. Review training methods periodically. Since the workplace isn't static, training methods should be evaluated often and enhanced, as needed. Remove dated material from the syllabus. It wastes time and can be confusing to the rookie, who already has a lot to learn.

2. Spotlight employee manuals. Most newly hired employees receive an employee manual and sign pledges indicating they read them. Examine the employee manual and if it contains information you believe should be highlighted, invite the rookie to spend some time with you to review specifics. It won't be surprising if the rookie has some questions about attendance, absenteeism, and holidays, and you might want to spotlight ethics policy. If someone in the Human Resource department routinely takes on this assignment, you need not repeat it unless you believe it could help a rookie to avoid making some mistakes.

3. Set the stage for bringing errors out into the open. If the rookie knows you think of mistakes as learning opportunities he or she should be forthright about revealing a mistake. No matter what the employee manual states regarding honesty and open-door policy, the rookie will be greatly influenced by experience. If he tells you, "I didn't Express Mail the contract to the Tidwell Brothers," and you say, "Contracts never leave our office any other way. What could you be thinking? This will never do. Draw up a duplicate contract and overnight it!" the rookie's experience will make him less likely to step forward quickly after he realizes he made a mistake. If, however, you respond, "That was a mistake but it's easily rectified. Draw up a duplicate contract and I'll telephone Bruce Tidwell to tell him it will be on his desk tomorrow. I'll ask him to destroy the other one when it arrives," you should achieve the immediate goal and pave the way for quick mending of future errors.

4. Don't pull out your magnifying glass because some rookies don't make errors. It's worth mentioning because it does happen. When a rookie turns in a top-notch performance day in and day out, don't ask yourself what he's doing wrong. Instead ask yourself, "how did I get so lucky?"

In a Word . . .

When you work with a rookie it's a little like working with a clean slate. This employee doesn't have a track record with your company. In order to bring the rookie up to speed, you're going to devote time to the training, coaching, motivating, and all-round grooming of this employee. Remember, that's the primary reason the rookie is mentioned in the negaholic category. No matter how quick this individual learns, no matter how many skills he or she brings to the workplace, the downside is that there is always a steep learning curve to be considered. Surely, the first steps the rookie takes are at the lowest end of the curve and you or another employee must slow down to work with the rookie. Pepper this employee's arrival with generous amounts of patience and reasonable expectations until the rookie is a rookie no more.

THE OVERLY SENSITIVE PERSON

THIS LABEL IS SOMETIMES used to put a person on the defensive, suggesting that something is wrong with the "sensitive" person and not with the individual who makes the accusation. It's often even a defense for harassment: "Oh, she can't be serious. I was just joking." That's not the topic for discussion here. For our purposes, overly sensitive employees are especially serious about their jobs, and it might be they take any criticism to heart and magnify it.

Here's a scenario: Sabrina tells Winston a client specifically asked for him. "He wants something fresh and new for the spring campaign. He'd like whatever you come up with to be set in the United States of America. He didn't care for the last video that featured people all around the globe. He asked me to tell you to keep it all in America." Being sought out by this client is a nice feather in Winston's cap, yet his delight fades quickly. "What do you mean he didn't care for the last video? He loved it when he first saw it." Winston broods. He slouches in his chair, paces the hallway and doesn't make eye contact with anyone. He doesn't read e-mails and doesn't return telephone calls.

"Here we go again," Winston's assistant mumbles.

PREDICTABLE PATTERN

Overly sensitive employees are
often late with their work.

Winston is focused on the wrong thing, but it's of no value to tell him so. He'll wallow in the doldrums for a time, and then snap out of it and get started on the new assignment. Sabrina has learned it's best to let him get over it without her intervention. Still, since it's difficult to anticipate what will upset him, it's often impossible to set and meet deadlines. Another artist on Sabrina's staff is overly sensitive, too. When this employee is upset, she arrives late and leaves early. When these employees feel appreciated they'll both work late or on weekends to get work done. And, they're both tough taskmasters, expecting the best from themselves.

WHERE'S THE HARM?

a. Income can be interrupted and diminished when jobs aren't finished on time. Customers are disappointed when promises are not kept in a timely fashion. You risk losing repeat business. Try totaling time-delays for a six-month period. Without so many delays, could more jobs have been accepted and completed? If so your company loses because overly sensitive employees fritter away time. (Are they occupied nursing their egos?)

b. Overly sensitive employees stomp out candid communication. Winston's boss and his secretary expect that he requires "special handling." Even though they might not consciously realize it, they measure everything they tell him. No one knows if or when this approach is costly for the company. Does this cramp in communication impede the development or exchange of ideas? These are the sorts of nagging questions that wander the back roads of your mind when you're calculating the cost of having an overly sensitive employee on staff. You probably don't know the answer in tangible terms, yet your gut guesses it's "yes."

c. Delay has a domino effect. When the artist turns over his work to the production people, and the production people rent time in a sound studio, hire an announcer, and the announcer reserves time for the job and says "no" to other jobs—well, you can see where this leads. Unless your overly sensitive employee works in a vacuum, colleagues and coworkers will be delayed, too. Cost overruns could result. Tempers might flare. Nothing good is likely to come of this kind of delay.

RECOMMENDATIONS

1. Offer need-to-know information. A quick mental screening might help you to avoid a damaging situation. Use your judgment ahead of time and filter out unnecessary details. For example, Sabrina didn't have to tell Winston the client "didn't like" something. Winston only needed to know the client wanted to focus on America.

2. Ask for frequent updates on work-in-progress as soon as you realize the overly sensitive employee is fretting and not working. (Read Chapter 6, The Procrastinator, for more tips.)

3. If a delay appears to be inevitable, put out the fire before it begins and inform anyone who will be held up. They can probably adjust schedules to minimize the inconvenience. This requires more of your time, but it's likely to save considerable time for others.

UNACCEPTABLE ATTITUDE

Overly sensitive employees are more likely to quit.

These employees aren't the count-your-blessings type. Because they can't process disappointments effectively, they might funnel themselves down the road to the door marked "Exit." Maybe it's because they don't know what else to do. If you can, provide opportunities for them to "let off steam" before they come to that conclusion. Of course, you won't do this unless you believe the person's skills and contributions to the company make them worth the bother.

Juanita stepped into Henri's office and said, "I'm no good at my job. No one here appreciates me. I quit." She was wearing her hat and coat and carrying a package that clearly contained the contents of her desk drawer. Henri knew she was an overly sensitive employee, but she was also the best wedding planner consultant the company had on staff.

"Maybe someday, Juanita, but not today," Henri said. "We're about to hire a new company to supply table linen. I won't sign the contract until you review the samples and give me your approval. A sample case awaits you in the conference room." Henri helped Juanita back away from her ultimatum. He didn't ask why, he didn't offer her a shoulder to cry on. He put her to work.

WHERE'S THE HARM?

a. The overly sensitive employee can leave you in the lurch. Juanita didn't step into Henri's office to give him two weeks notice. She was prepared to walk out the door. His clever response saved the day. If you work with a small team of people, if one of them makes a quick exit it can be especially shattering. Ironically, although this person doesn't want to be a bother and is alarmed at the thought of it, he or she will be the one to walk out on you at the drop of a hat.

b. The overly sensitive employee isn't leadership material. A leader needs a thick skin. The overly sensitive employee who is thin-skinned and easily hurt doesn't measure up for the position. If you must assign this individual a leadership role, make it a shared position. Just be absolutely sure the coleader isn't overly sensitive, too. Hopefully, the second person will help maintain a balance: "Oh, Charlie. You didn't do anything wrong. Ms. Carol talks that way to everyone."

In affect, the coleader supplies the voice-of-reason and helps to keep the overly sensitive employee centered. You might want to try copartnering the overly sensitive employee with an easy-going coworker on all assignments, no matter whether they're leadership positions or not. These two people might work together better than if the overly sensitive person did the job alone. If or when the ploy is not successful, don't be too quick to fault the copartner. You already know it's not easy to reason with this overly sensitive individual.

c. The overly sensitive employee is self-centered. Consider how this individual disrupts actions and involves others in the process, and you may conclude it's-all-about-them. Even if they are generous, giving individuals under other circumstances, this aspect of their personalities results in selfish actions. Accordingly, he or she doesn't set out to offend you, but it happens. It might be easier for you to shrug off the offense when you recognize it's unintentional. Let's say you have an overly sensitive employee who gets up from a meeting and walks out, apparently thinking nothing of it. Then he comes to you afterward and says: "I didn't mean to keep you waiting, boss. I just had to get out of the meeting. Johnson was saying ugly things and I didn't want to listen."

The fact that you get an apology is a good sign! If this type of employee comes forward on his or her own and initiates an apology, it suggests that there might be more progress to follow. Sometimes just an apology is not nearly enough if an employee has done something very wrong. You should never minimize the importance of an apology in a more minor situation such as the one above. Don't just fluff things off, either. Pause for a moment and comment; this will let your overly sensitive type know that the apology did not go unnoticed.

RECOMMENDATIONS

1. Remind the overly sensitive employee of how his/her actions impact the company. "We're counting on you, Harris, to help put us on the map this year. Do you realize that each member of the sales team plays a vital role? If we maintain one for all, all for one attitudes, no one can beat us!" Send a note, say it, and announce it at meetings. Keep reminding Harris that he's not flying solo and others count on him. Rely on his overly sensitive nature to respond favorably to this frequent reminder. (Like chicken soup, it can't hurt!)

2. Use motivational signs. "Quitting Is Not an Option" is direct and to the point. Surround your overly sensitive employee with messages to which he or she can relate. This individual has probably thought of quitting. Motivational expressions or messages inserted in company newsletters and similar resources (such as tag lines on intercompany e-mail) usually don't cost much and speak to everyone. Okay, maybe "Quitting Is Not an Option" is incredibly blunt. But the point is, in an instance like this one, you need to show this employee that quibbling over these sorts of issues is not acceptable. Your job is to help this employee to get on with things. Overly sensitive people are prone to exaggeration, and one of the best ways to temper that exaggeration is to put them back on task. If after trying you can't get your overly sensitive type to move on with things, then you'll have to consider whether you can continue to have them as part of your team, and then act accordingly.

3. If you truly accept the two-heads-are-better-than-one theory, then sell it. It's easy to be enthusiastic about something you believe, and enthusiasm is contagious. If the overly sensitive employee knows you're a proponent of this method for achieving goals, he'll view it as standard operating procedure. He probably won't notice that you lean toward the buddy system approach with him more than with anyone else. And, should he ask about it you can respond, "You're an outstanding work partner. I believe in taking advantage of a good thing. Why would we change what works?"

In a Word . . .

Sometimes, you're dumbfounded by what sends this individual off in a huff. The overly sensitive person easily misunderstands statements since he or she appears to be turned inward. "It's all about me, me, me." You're well advised to remind this employee frequently how important his or her performance is to the others: "We work best when we work together." Break it down to specifics so that it's useable information. For example, "Jill is relying on your figures to finalize the inventory report," or "Emily tells me your graphic arts contributions to the directory helped make it the best directory we ever produced. Nice teamwork!" Don't be stingy with explanations, since the overly sensitive person might need to be introduced to the idea that not every statement is intended to affect her or him. Try using statements such as: "When Ken said he was angry, he wasn't angry with you. He was angry because he wasn't going to meet the deadline."

THE MANIPULATOR

A MANIPULATOR IS an artful bully. Instead of intimidating or tormenting coworkers, the manipulator cajoles and maneuvers them to suit his or her desires. You didn't see the last of bullies when you left school days behind, and you didn't see the last of manipulators either. Be on guard for this type's more subtle stunts. The manipulator is likely to be very comfortable with his or her long-established pattern of behavior.

Manuel told his new supervisor that he needed to work overtime or risk disappointing a customer. Manuel calculated he could earn an additional thousand dollars annually if he worked overtime five times a year, and that's what he did.

When his new supervisor responded, "Let's review that work order together and see how we can avoid overtime," Manuel was stunned. When he couldn't manipulate this new supervisor to do his bidding, he began to think about quitting. He was a skilled furniture maker and knew he could get a job elsewhere.

PREDICTABLE PATTERN

The manipulator doesn't like to take "no" for an answer.

When people resist a manipulator, he or she isn't likely to respond gracefully. Some manipulators make threats, shout demands, and even hurl insults. Manuel's thought of quitting constitutes a threat, but it's a threat with teeth in it. He believes he will get another job with ease. The new supervisor may not have a clue that Manuel is a manipulator, but she's probably about to find out. These people are easier to identify when you say "no" because that's when they shift into high gear to get their way. (Manuel might say, "I can't believe you'd question my judgment. The other supervisor never did that. She believed in me!") Manipulators rarely have regard for anyone's needs or wishes other than their own.

WHERE'S THE HARM?

a. A manipulator is always suspected of having an ulterior motive. Coworkers assume the manipulator wants something. They expect to come out on the losing side of the exchange. Charlene is always asking folks to "cover" for her. She either needs to leave early to attend to a compelling personal matter ("I promised to help make funeral arrangements for my friend's aunt," or "I'll only leave forty minutes early to meet my friend," she says). She's also inclined to take extended lunch breaks ("My stomach can't handle a rushed lunch," she insists).

She always has a new and interesting story and claims she doesn't want the boss to know her business. "You're a pal, Loretta, I can trust you." When questioned, Loretta is vague in her responses about the "missing"

Charlene. But, Charlene has no problem saying to the boss, "Didn't Loretta tell you I left early?"

The next time Charlene asks for a favor, Loretta says "no," only to find herself on the receiving end of Charlene's verbal abuse. Coworkers get the message. They try to avoid the manipulator, and even when she has something completely benign on her mind, they assume the worst.

b. A manipulator won't share the load. Even when a manipulator is a skilled employee, the focus is not on what can he do for the company. This employee is self-centered, won't offer to lend a hand, and doesn't know the meaning of the word reciprocity.

RECOMMENDATIONS

1. Don't give in when you know you're correct. When Manuel's new supervisor wanted to avoid scheduling overtime hours Manuel was quick to whine and make accusations in response. He was even ready to quit. Most people don't like to be confronted with unpleasantness and will acquiesce to establish harmony. When a manager waffles, compromises, or backs down, it's like giving the manipulator a green light to go for it! Managers and coworkers who are sure their positions are correct are better able to stand firm and not be manipulated!

2. Take time to listen. It's tempting to anticipate the manipulator's motives but best to listen to this person as though they're starting with a clean slate each time they approach you. Does the manipulator have a legitimate concern? Is her my-way-or-the-highway attitude based upon something valid? Listen. Ask questions that can't be answered with one-word answers, and size up the situation. You might actually find you're sometimes in agreement with this employee's requests or observations. Listen, too, for indications that a manipulator has put another employee on the spot. Make it clear that Charlene, for example, cannot leave early without notifying you.

3. When you differ, deliver the message in simple sentences. It's likely you'll have to repeat yourself. State facts: "Sorry, but the policy has changed. No overtime work will be approved" or "Repeated tardiness is cause for dismissal. It's discussed in the employee handbook." If the conversation goes around and around, and you and the manipulator both sound like broken records, stop. Try saying, "I have a meeting to go to and can't discuss this further now," or "I have to submit a budget request before 3:00 P.M. I've got to give that my attention now." If possible, don't offer another time to meet apropos this issue. A repeated, easy-to-understand message has been delivered. There's nothing more to add.

If the manipulator asks to meet with you again, you'll have little choice, but you can change the meeting dynamics. Invite your own boss to participate or, ask the Human Resources manager to join you. When another person is added to the discussion, the manipulator might be inclined to hang up the boxing gloves. The manipulator prefers one-on-one meetings when he or she isn't sure of coming out on top.

SNEAKY SCHEME

Manipulators like an appreciative audience.

The manipulator is rarely a shy, retiring type and doesn't strive to keep differences under wraps. This person usually thinks very highly of him or herself and likes to put on a show. It's not hard to imagine this sort thinking things like, "Won't they think I'm bold?" or "They'll love the way I get the boss to turn beet red."

Ray wanted to switch places with Herman at the sorting table. "I'm left-handed, Herman. I need to be at the end." Ray had a point, but Herman was so annoyed with him over previous encounters, he wasn't willing to give an inch.

"Look at this everyone," Ray announced to the four other mine workers standing at the table, "Herman's so stupid he can't figure out that I belong at the end." The other men stopped their work and looked at Ray.

"He always has to have things his way," Herman announced to no one in particular as he changed places with Ray. Ray was just getting started. "I'm stepping out for a smoke. Come on guys, join me." Herman didn't smoke, but the others did, and they left the sorting table to step outside with Ray.

Moments passed, and the manager approached Herman. "You know the rule, Herman, it's against safety regulations for anyone to work at the sorting table alone." The manager cut the power that moved the conveyor belt. "Wait for the others to return," he ordered.

When they returned, Ray pushed the power switch. "Poor Herman couldn't be trusted," he teased.

Herman stormed off looking for the manager. "That guy is a clown and I can't work with him," he complained. The manager wanted to tell Herman to cool down. He knew all about Ray and his act. "Don't let him get to you, Herman. Go work in the packing room for the rest of the afternoon."

WHERE'S THE HARM?

a. Someone has to be the babysitter. The manipulator will often bully or bait someone in front of others in order to attract attention. The manager can usually see through this maneuver and will have to decide on a course of action. No matter what other steps are necessary, it's reasonably certain the manager will have to offer tea and sympathy to someone.

b.   There's rarely a dull moment. Sometimes it's nice to have dull, uneventful periods when work is humming along without incident. When a manipulator who enjoys performing for an audience is in the area, chances are it won't be long before the show will go on. The boss might want to take steps that support dull moments. One way to do this is to remove the audience. Give the manipulator work that must be done solo. If possible, you might also want to arrange for this person to telecommute one or two days a week. If the manipulator can work from home at tasks that are measurable so that you know work is being done, why not give this arrangement a try?

c.   Employees take time out to witness the entertainment. Many people like to watch a cat-and-mouse game as long as they're not participating. When Ray baited Herman, the others didn't speak out. They also didn't focus on their work. They were completely distracted from their sorting-table activities. A manipulator's antics usually cost the company productivity time.

RECOMMENDATIONS

1.   Show up when the manipulator is performing. Your mere presence can act like water on a fire. And you can participate. "Sorry. We can't have everyone leave the sorting table at the same time. You can relay out in sets of two. That way, we won't have one person at the table, which you know is against security rules."

2. Tally the times you spend diverted from other tasks. Sometimes it seems like an eternity when someone makes life tedious. What happens when it is an eternity? You can put things in perspective when you have facts and figures. If the manipulator costs you an extra thirty minutes a week that might be acceptable. It might be unacceptable, however, if the manipulator costs you a day or two each month. You might decide to cut this person's hours or dismiss this person. You'll make a well-informed decision when you have the facts and don't rely solely upon what seems like an eternity.

In a Word . . .

The manipulator is a meddler, and you can't turn away from this individual even for a short while. This employee's Modus Operandi is to ponder: Where's the angle? What can I do to grab attention? The manipulator might try to take charge of a situation just for the heck of it. He or she doesn't always gain very much for the effort. You've got to be alert to possible shenanigans for the sake of harmony within the department and for the sake of achieving goals. You're not running a playground. If you and others in the department aren't able to subdue the manipulator successfully, you may want to issue marching papers to this individual. At the least, you'll want to calculate this employee's value to the company and ask yourself, "Is it worth it?"

COMMUNICATION: THE UPSIDE AND THE DOWNSIDE

Master the Fine Art of Effective Communication

EFFECTIVE COMMUNICATION is key to managing difficult people, and this chapter is devoted to widely respected communication principles. It's important to mention, however, that mastering the fine art of communication is a lifelong pursuit. The following information is not and cannot be considered complete. It's valuable information and should add to your store of knowledge, but it comes with a warning: Don't stop here. Each day the sun rises, you have the opportunity to sharpen your communication skills.

The Components of Good Communication

When we think about communication, we think about being able to express ourselves so that others understand both our words and our intentions. When we speak, it's estimated that words are only a small percentage of the typical communication process—just 7 percent. Body language and nonverbal cues account for 55 percent, while 38 percent comes through in the tone of voice. When we write, these components are missing, and so the process differs.

SPEAKING TO ONE ANOTHER

The communication cycle is a back-and-forth process, with each participant talking and listening. The exchanges are sometimes lengthy, sometimes rapid-fire. Listening is every bit as important as talking. The problem is, we tend to spend listening time thinking about what we're going to say next, what we should cook for dinner, whether those concert tickets are still available, when the cat's next set of shots is due . . . We focus on anything and everything except what the other person is saying.

You could be anxious about making your points when it comes your turn to speak. And it could be your brain's fault—not your mind, but your brain. Often, our mouths step ahead of our brains because our brains haven't had enough time to process information as we receive it or rethink a more appropriate response as additional information flows in.

Just as there is more to speaking than the words you utter, there is more to listening than the sounds that enter your ears. Sometimes the real message lies in what's not being said. It's important to listen between the lines to hear the unspoken messages. Pay attention to unspoken signals and nonverbal cues. When an employee says, "Yes, I'd be happy to research that information," but her voice is high-pitched and tense, and she crosses her arms across her chest before she speaks, what is she really telling you? She may be sending a message that she has enough work already without tackling another time-consuming assignment, that she's cold and wishes she'd brought her sweater to the meeting, or that she can't stand the database librarian she'll have to contact to request the information. You can't know without asking questions, but you should know there's more to her response than the spoken words.

Effective listening is an activity that requires your full and focused attention:

• **Engage your mind to slow down your brain.** Let it hear every word as if it were a delightful chocolate that you want to savor until it melts away and every molecule of flavor seeps into your senses.

• **Beware of the familiarity trap.** As soon as the words begin to sound familiar, the search for new information ends. "I've heard this before!" your mind says, and it turns its attention elsewhere. Bring it back!

• **Don't cross the line from anticipation to assumption.** Anticipating someone's response or next question often helps you shape your end of the communication. But there's a fine line between anticipating and assuming, and assuming will almost always get you in trouble.

• **Maintain and keep eye contact, just as when you're speaking.** This shows that you're listening and demonstrates your sincerity. It also helps you pick up on nonverbal cues.

• **Don't formulate your response or mentally argue while the person is still speaking.** You can't be listening to someone else if you're busy listening to yourself.

Listening effectively doesn't mean you should allow conversations to roam where they will. You can, and often should, shape the direction of dialogue (at least in a business context). Use natural pauses to ask questions or make comments that redirect the conversation back to its intended purpose. Learn when to set aside that kindergarten rule you've assimilated so you can interrupt smoothly and effectively. Ask structured, open-ended questions to frame the subject, yet allow the person to respond freely. For instance: "What happened when you opened the box and discovered that all the templates were reversed?"

WRITING TO ONE ANOTHER

No discussion of communication is complete without mentioning the importance of effective writing skills. At some point, everyone in a company, no matter what their position or level, has to put his or her thoughts or comments on paper. You might need to write a memo, a report, or a performance appraisal. What you say matters; how you say it can matter more. Although writing is a life skill, not just a job skill, many people turn into babbling bureaucrats when they write. There's no reason for business writing to be any more convoluted than talking. In fact, it can be easier to write because you focus just on your presentation. It's as easy as three steps that you can view as your AIM:

1. *Audience.* Who will read your message?

2. *Intent.* Why are you writing?

3. *Message.* What do you have to say?

Make separate lists to answer each of these three questions. Then use your lists as an outline and begin writing. Write as though your audience is sitting in front of you and remember:

• **You don't have to start at the beginning.** For some managers, the best way to begin writing is to start with what's on their minds. You can rearrange blocks of words after you get them down on paper (or on screen). Word processing programs and computers make this very easy. Often, one idea flows into the next once you get started, leading you through to the end.

• **Writing is a process of editing and revision.** Nothing is ever a one-shot deal. If you don't like the way something sounds, change it.

• **Every sentence should be relevant to your intended message.** Keep your audience in mind. The myriad details of last month's focus group might fascinate you, but the employees receiving your report just need to know what problems exist and suggestions for remedying them.

• **You should write as though you are talking.** Hold the slang, but stay conversational. Write enough content (your message) to cover your intent—no more. Be sure the vocabulary you choose is appropriate for your audience; steer clear of jargon. When you're finished writing, save your file or set your paper aside. Go get a drink of water, take a short walk, and talk to an employee. When you return to your desk, read your writing aloud. Are there places where you stumble? Choose a different word or rephrase the section. Compare what you'd say in person to what you've written. Keep at it until you can read your words aloud without faltering.

Don't let the process of writing intimidate you. It's just another form of communication.

SETTING THE RIGHT EXAMPLE

Your body is not always your friend when it comes to communication. It has a mind of its own, so to speak—or rather, it escapes the influence of your mind, which is busy regulating the words that leave your mouth. So your body is pretty much on its own, and it doesn't always tell the same story as your words. Maybe your eyes wander to the computer screen rather than remaining focused on the person in front of you, your arms cross, and your foot starts to jiggle.

Your words say, "You did a great job with the presentation. I've had phone calls from several people saying how much they enjoyed it." But your body's sending different signals: "Man, is she ever going to leave? There's that e-mail from Sarah I've been waiting for, I have a conference call in ten minutes, and Rob wants that preliminary budget from me." Meanwhile, there's poor Alice pouring out her angst, eager for you to tell her she's doing great, which you are. But she's not believing you, because of your body language. Which message would you heed if you were sitting in Alice's chair?

Smile if you must, but the fact is, unless you perfect your communication skills—including your body language—you're probably setting a poor example for employees to follow. If the scenario just described could apply to you, it's time for a change! Improve your skills and become a model for others to emulate.

If Alice's boss applies the following rules the next time she's in his office, she's likely to exit dancing:

• **Maintain eye contact with the person to whom you're talking.** It's okay to look away now and then; you don't want to create the impression that this is a stare-down.

• **Don't fold your arms across your chest or cross your legs.** These are classic defensive postures that delivers the message, "Don't mess with me." Rarely is this message appropriate in the workplace. Let your arms rest on your chair if you're seated. When standing, many people fold their arms because they don't know what else to do with them; it feels awkward just to let them hang at your sides. Practice. It doesn't look as bad as it feels.

- **Don't sit across from someone.** This can feel confrontational, especially if you are behind a desk or at a table. Unless there's a reason for you to maintain an image of power (and sometimes there is), sit next to the person instead.

- **Don't fidget or fiddle around with things.** This includes sighing and playing with your hair (including mustache and beard), jewelry, or pens and pencils. Don't practice your origami skills with pieces of paper you find on your desk, or craft paperclip sculptures. Such actions are distracting. Any train of thought is likely to leave without you if you're concentrating on how to transform a memo into a swan.

- **Gestures are often space-fillers.** Are you waving your hands around to try to paint an air picture of something, or are you having trouble finding the right words? It's usually more effective to use a pencil and paper to sketch out your picture, or simply to pause for a moment to let the right words come to you. If you usually don't use *any* gestures, use some. It's hard to listen to a talking head, no matter how interested you are in the message.

- **Speak at a moderate pace.** When you speak, it should be not too fast, not too slow. Also be sure to enunciate.

- **Vary the tone and pitch of your voice.** Some people drone on in a monotone when speaking to a group, even though their conversational voices are friendly and full of personality. It's as though a little switch in their vocal cords flips and the vocal cords can emit sound on just a single frequency. One way to practice modulating your voice is to change the outgoing message on your voice mail daily. Strive for a different tone each day and attempt to sound interested in the caller, even though you're not there to take the call.

COMMUNICATING WITH YOUR STAFF

It's amazing how many managers barely interact with other employees. This creates discomfort on both sides. Some of this stems from the way American businesses select managers. Those who excel in their job skills are promoted to management positions to reward them for their abilities. Some of these workers, although terrific accountants, programmers, and production workers, are not people-people. As managers, they remain focused on doing a good job, failing to recognize that it now means helping everyone else do a good job, too.

Employees need you to stop around every morning (or at the beginning of the shift) to say hello. When you don't, they might assume something is wrong or feel ignored. And when you don't interact with your employees, you begin to assume that they think and act in certain ways. From these assumptions, you draw conclusions that they're doing, or not doing, certain things. Nature abhors a vacuum. When we don't have information, we make it up. This is true for managers and employees alike.

Consistent daily interaction promotes more than just good feelings; it also promotes effective and collaborative teamwork. When the manager takes a few moments to chat, employees feel better about coming to work and about doing the work expected of them.

SMALL TALK IS SIGNIFICANT

When you stop to ask employees what they did over the weekend, how things are with the kids, or mention a movie you saw, employees feel that you care about them as people and not just as cogs in the corporate machine. We need to remind each other that we are human and have lives outside of work. Small talk helps to create bonds.

Is small talk hard for you? That's okay. Communication is a craft each of us must perfect. Although the ability to talk seems natural enough, circumstances that require structured dialogue can make otherwise competent adults sputter incoherently. So consider small talk just one of the new skills you must learn to excel at your job as a manager. Each day, make it a point to:

• **Stop to greet employees by name.** Use the name the person uses when contacting you. If the employee's name is Michael, his coworkers call him Mike, and his wife calls him Mitch but he says, "This is Michael" when he calls you, then call him Michael. Names often reflect a level of trust and equity. Don't use an informal variation if it makes the employee uncomfortable.

• **Ask each employee one question related to a personal interest.** Yes, this might require you to do a little research. Careful listening can help you build a mental "information file" about each employee. "How was your weekend?" can elicit an astonishing breadth and depth of information.

• **Ask each employee one work-related question.** If this is new behavior for you, employees might react with suspicion, thinking you're checking up on them (which you are, in a sense) or something is wrong (which it probably isn't). As employees realize this is part of your daily routine, they'll warm up. The first sign of progress is when they start telling you about things that are going wrong; you know you're in your groove when they start telling you about things that are going right.

• **Go from office to office, cubicle to cubicle, workstation to workstation to make contact with employees.** Don't miss anyone; if you do, these people will feel slighted, or believe that something is wrong. If someone's not there for your rounds, touch base with him or her later in the day, however briefly. Ask questions, and listen to answers. Walk around and just listen to employees talk as they work. Don't sneak around—you want people to know you're there and you're interested.

The CEO's Mood Tells a Tale

Creative Computer Corporation's 600 employees worked on multiple floors in an office complex, yet everyone knew what kind of mood the CEO was in every day. If he walked around and stopped to talk with department managers, employees knew that the stock market was at least stable and product was moving smoothly through the production and distribution loops. If the CEO stayed in his office all day, emerging only to snap at his secretary, then employees recognized something was wrong. The market was down, beta testing revealed an unexpected bug, or focus groups didn't like the company's latest brainchild. Because almost everyone had stock options, employees feared the CEO's mood affected them directly—and this turned out to be true more often than not.

Employees are highly sensitive to routine, and to changes in it. They learn very quickly to read the moods of their managers, and to shape their own moods accordingly. One person's moods can influence the mood of others in a department or an entire company.

The bottom line is, you're communicating with your staff whether you like it or not. So take control of your actions and send messages that help everybody to succeed.

OPEN-DOOR POLICY

The open door is both literal and symbolic. If you tell employees they can come to talk with you any time but you work with your door closed, you are sending a mixed message. Most people see closed doors as stop signs. From childhood, we're trained not to enter without knocking, and we often hesitate to knock unless the need to talk to the person on the other side can't wait. Sometimes managers close doors out of habit or to block distractions. Even if you truly do want people to open the door and come in, many will be reluctant to do so. Unless you're working on something that requires privacy, leave your door open. The only way people know you have an open-door policy is if your door really is open.

OPEN DOOR: WHO SAYS SO?

When Mark became manager of the assembly group, he established what he believed was an effective open-door policy. He would see any employee about any matter—as long as the employee scheduled an appointment through his secretary and could provide evidence that he or she had already tried to resolve the concern. Initially, employees welcomed Mark's approach. The group's previous manager only talked to people who were in some sort of trouble and kept group meetings focused on discussions of work tasks. Within the first few months, almost every employee had scheduled an appointment to talk with Mark. While he was friendly enough in these one-on-one meetings, he expected people to present a one-to three-minute summary of the problem and the steps the employee had taken to try to resolve it. He had little interest in casual conversation, and no interest in matters that weren't directly related to work processes or results.

Not surprisingly, appointments soon dropped off. Mark interpreted this as an indication the group had come together as a smooth functioning team capable of troubleshooting without running to him. But the employees grew increasingly dissatisfied. At least their previous manager had made it unmistakably clear that she had no interest in them and their problems. Mark gave all the appearances of being interested, but in the end was no more so than his predecessor. Requiring appointments to see Mark meant that his "open" door was shut tight. Although Mark believed he was available, his rules and procedures made him inaccessible.

Managers set the tone for their work groups or departments. Employees need to know they really can come to you whenever they feel they need to, not just when you determine it's appropriate for them to do so. Of course, this means you'll find yourself listening to personal problems, family matters, and petty disagreements. But that's all part of being a manager—that parent hat gets a lot of wear.

CONSTRUCTIVE CRITICISM

Feedback is the sort of buzzword that has different meanings. In electronics, it's undesirable sound distortion. In the workplace, it's one person giving another person a reaction or response—one that sometimes sounds like the annoying whines and screeches we associate with electronic feedback. In communication, all too often feedback becomes synonymous with criticism. And criticism (i.e., disapproval) is unwelcome.

Under ideal circumstances, feedback is a loop—a cycle of action and reaction. Neither needs to be big or significant. In fact, when feedback becomes a communication loop, most people don't notice that it's even taking place.

You can deliver constructive criticism matter-of-factly in a positive light. People constantly seek feedback from their managers. Some ask for it directly: "How did I do?" Others are less direct: "What did the client say?" Although conventional wisdom preaches that no news is good news, in the corporate world the reverse is more often the case. Or at least that's what employees think, as they fret and worry because they haven't heard anything from you.

Stop by an employee's workstation to offer congratulations on a report well written or a project completed ahead of schedule. Ask if there's some way to get the figures to the accounting department a day earlier or with fewer errors. Constructive criticism will roll off your tongue like congratulations when the feedback loop is in good working order.

When giving feedback, including criticism, be concrete. Cite specific, tangible examples:

1. "More orders have come in for that new gizmo you designed than for any new product we've debuted." Or, "Orders have dropped off on that new gizmo you designed. Reports in the newspaper tell potential consumers it has a weak component. Can that component be strengthened?"

2. "I saw how you calmed that angry woman by getting her out of the waiting room and into your office where she could regain her composure." Or, "I know you were trying to calm that angry woman by getting her to a quiet place to regain her composure, but you put the company at risk by taking her into your private office. If this circumstance arises again, promise me please, you'll get a third party to join you so that you're not alone."

3. "Josephine Hall is a major client, and your follow-up call caught an error in her order before she noticed it. She

called me to say how courteous and professional you are on the phone. She received the corrected order by next-day delivery, which averted a potential crisis." Or, "Josephine Hall is a major client, and your follow-up call caught an error in her order before she noticed it. She was delighted with your efforts and etiquette, but you neglected to tell me about the problem. I wasn't able to respond intelligently when she called. Please keep me informed of errors especially when dealing with a major client."

Work Style Is Worth Noting

Some employees require constant direction, feedback, and redirection. Others are better left to a general framework within which they are free to structure the job's tasks, flow, and progress measures. Consider how each employee works most productively. When possible, shape your criticism to fit within the context of the employee's work style.

Sometimes an employee's work style is the primary factor in performance and production matters. New employees and seasoned employees with job responsibilities that depart from previous experience might be struggling to find a good match between work style and assignments. Offer suggestions for trying different approaches to help the employee find ways to achieve better outcomes.

Consider this an incremental process; no one makes major changes overnight. If you see a pattern emerging, divvy up your feedback to cover one facet at a time. If the issue is time management, you might cover establishing timelines this week and prioritizing next week. This is a work in progress, and results won't necessarily be consistent. Be patient. This is the most important kind of shaping, and it's well worth your time and effort.

Look at your own work style and be sure that the criticism you're offering is relevant to the employee and how he or she works, not a comparison or criticism because the employee's work style differs from yours.

Tips for Giving Constructive Criticism

When offering constructive criticism, keep the following points in mind:

• Comment on specific actions and behaviors: "Barb was very upset that you yelled at her and then hung up on her over the delay at the print shop," works better than "Johnson, you're an insensitive boor!"

• Whenever practical, give feedback that is specific yet offers choices: "In reading this report, I didn't get a sense for what the product does. Would you please restructure the introduction or add another section to part two?"

• Look for ways to frame less-than-positive feedback in the context of realistic improvement. This is not about sugarcoating; most people resent attempts to cloak bad news in the trappings of compliments. "Customer complaints about delivery delays are up 35 percent this quarter. Let's take a look at the reasons for the delays and then brainstorm for solutions."

THE GOOD GUYS

Some managers want to be good guys so they give only positive feedback, at the drop of a hat. It doesn't take employees long to figure out that when praise is always forthcoming, its value diminishes. When feedback is initially positive, but a contradictory message follows, the feedback is less helpful. If the news is bad, just deliver it. Your employees are adults; they know they make mistakes and that life is not all roses and chocolate. When less-than-positive feedback involves just one or two people, deliver it individually and in private. When you have a message for the entire group, be direct but compassionate. Don't single out individuals in the group setting. If you have additional specific comments, deliver them in private.

TO-THE-RESCUE TIPS FOR RESOLVING COMMUNICATION ISSUES

Glitches in employee communication need attention. Sometimes you'll introduce the ounce of prevention that's worth a pound of cure. Other times, you must act after an issue surfaces. Be aware of the following points:

1. Bringing the right employees together: The only people who should be at a meeting of any size are people who have a specific reason for being there. Make a list of the people you're planning to include, and write down what contribution you expect each to make. If you can't identify a specific contribution, scratch the person from your list.

2. Regulating the flow of a meeting that's underway: If a few employees begin to dominate a meeting, intercede and call on silent employees. Pull out your parent hat for a few minutes and let the group know that all members have something to contribute, and all are welcome to participate.

3. Maintaining a balance: If an employee is barraged with questions or criticisms, step in to put an end to it. You're having a meeting, not an inquisition.

If employees see that those who stick out their necks end up getting their heads chopped off, they're not likely to speak up, even when the topic concerns them. There's a balance between open dialogue and abuse.

4. Moderating differences at any time: Sometimes differences collide. Each person feels strongly about his or her perspective, and the situation lands in your lap. Put your communication skills to work negotiating solutions all parties accept and respect. This way, no one comes away feeling like a winner or a loser.

5. Diffusing anger: Sometimes tempers flare and people lose it. Little things add up, tensions and frustrations build. People feel powerless to control or change situations they believe should be different but exist because you (or some other person or department) intentionally created the circumstances. Whether or not there is truth to this perception doesn't matter. Anger is an intense and powerful blend of emotion and action, which often frightens even the person who is angry. Act to defuse anger quickly. If necessary, tell people to take a timeout and disperse.

6. Tackling one thing at a time: Break issues down into manageable components. Armies use a "divide and conquer" tactic with great success, and it will work for you, too. Try to engage the employee to help identify components and suddenly the two of you are on the same side!

7. Forging a common allegiance: Working toward common goals establishes a connection defined by similarities, not differences. When both sides want to achieve the same outcomes, they're often more willing to search for common ground. Help employees to recognize common goals.

8. Being there: Often, by getting involved you interrupt the cycle and start turning things around. You represent a fresh start; there is no pattern of behavior the person feels compelled to continue with you. Even if someone comes storming into your office, there's usually a trail of angry words left behind.

9. Listening actively: Let the person fully explain his or her position and frustration, even if you think you already know what the problem is or have heard it before. Ask questions only to clarify details, but let the full story be told.

Group Dynamics and Conflict Resolution

FAMILIES EVOLVE AND GROW through marriages, births, and adoptions, frequently bringing people with disparate interests and personalities together. Workplaces are similar. Often, people who have quite different personalities are thrown together simply because they've chosen the same career path. Coworkers spend more time with each other than they do with the people they have chosen to be in their lives, such as spouses, significant others, and good friends. Just as family members don't always get along or even like each other, neither do employees.

Whether employees like each other or not, it's still important for them to be able to work together. Forging viable working relationships among employees isn't always easy, though. The most effective way for a manager to bring people together in collaboration and cooperation is to stay focused on the job's requirements and how well employees complete those tasks. This helps them—and you—to tolerate personality differences. It also requires outstanding communication skills. (See Chapters 14 and 17.)

Despite a manager's best efforts, encouraging employees who don't like each other to work together harmoniously isn't always successful. When all attempts fail, don't insist that those people work together. Period. In most cases, however, there are methods and strategies to help you avoid that type of situation.

SYSTEM VS. PEOPLE PROBLEMS

Problems within a work group can result from personal issues, system issues, or both. Sometimes the source of the problem is obvious: The design group can't complete the final drawings for a project because the software update they need to install first is backordered from the manufacturer. The customer call center can't improve wait times and loses calls because there are too few lines to handle the volume of incoming calls. The production department is ready to roll, but the templates were cut wrong and the manager had to send them back to the supplier. These are clearly systems problems; employees are ready and eager to do what needs to be done, but they don't have what they need to move forward.

At other times, the system hits a glitch because people aren't functioning optimally. For example, the Gizmo Master Corporation prided itself on listening to its customers and using customer feedback to shape new products and services. An important part of the marketing representative's job was to follow up with customers at certain intervals after sales closed, to make sure customers were satisfied and to solicit suggestions for improvements. Customers often offered good ideas for new products and services. The marketing reps passed these ideas on to the product development department.

The product development engineers were less than impressed. In fact, over time they became angry at the marketing reps. It wasn't easy coming up with the next best-selling gizmo, and the engineers resented the implication that "just anybody" could zip something off the top of his head and magically create the company's next claim to fame. There were computer models and prototypes and lab tests and field tests and focus groups . . . followed by more of the same after revisions and reconfigurations. Then, *maybe* an idea might make it into production, if the legal department gave its approval.

Marketing accused product development of failing to make good on the company's promise to listen to its customers. Product development charged that marketing had no concept of the manpower and other resources it required to explore, let alone develop, the ideas customers suggested. Egos clashed as colleagues crossed into each other's turf. Marketing took heat from customers because the new products they wanted weren't yet available. Product development got flack from upper management because customers were unhappy.

Without intervention, such battles spiral out of control, ultimately interfering with the company's goals. Clearly, this system is flawed: Marketing is gathering information it is not empowered to use. Policies and procedures, although useful and appropriate in many circumstances, prevent product development from reaching beyond its boundaries. And the employees clearly contribute to the problem: Marketing reps make promises they can't keep, alienating customers. Product development engineers feel threatened and become defensive.

FINDING A SOLUTION

This problem escalated to the point where one morning, the managers of these two departments finally shut themselves in a conference room until they were able to emerge with a plan. They created a new work group, with members from each department, to bridge the differences between the departments. Over several months, this group developed a new set of policies and procedures that defined the needs of the production department so the marketing reps could solicit customer feedback the engineers could use. These new procedures called for a quarterly meeting among selected customers, marketing reps, and product development engineers to discuss ideas for new products and services. The bridge team presented the policies and procedures to a meeting of both departments and worked through a series of revisions until both groups could support them. Six months after implementing the new framework, productivity in both departments was up and customer complaints dropped. By year's end, the company exceeded its sales goals.

Personal issues typically arise from personality conflicts or performance problems. Sometimes people just don't get along with each other. Though we like to believe that adults can put aside their differences to work toward common goals, this doesn't always happen. Sometimes, the challenge is isolating the personalities that are clashing—not always as easy as it sounds—so they can try to work out their differences. In other situations, colleagues might get along fine (or even too well) but lack the skills or the competence to do the job properly. In general, ruling out systems problems points the finger at people problems.

MAINTAINING HARMONY

While everyone working for a company might be likened to an entire extended family, a work group might be considered a small gathering of relatives. People are forced into relationships with each other that otherwise might not exist, and while they often get along just fine, sometimes there are problems. It's important for you, the manager, to have your finger on the pulse of your team at all times so you'll immediately know when things run off track.

Once a situation escalates it can be too late to salvage the group, at least in terms of restoring it to its previous level of collaboration and productivity. It's not enough to peek in at people a few times during the day to see if things look all right. You need to monitor output and attitudes consistently.

If there is a team problem, you need to get people to talk. Depending on the nature of the problem, you might meet first with the entire group or with members individually. As soon as you figure out what's going on, take action. It's usually also a good idea to follow up with a group meeting to discuss the nature of the problem, how it's being addressed, when you expect to see things change, what changes you expect to see, and what role, if any, other group members have in resolving it. Avoid naming individuals unless there is no other way to talk about the situation. If you must use names, be sure to focus on behaviors and events, not people.

Get ready to put on your parent, conflict-resolution and cheerleader hats. You need to take decisive action, yet at the same time help group members to see each other's perspectives. Sometimes the staff members involved in the conflict will have to transfer to another department or leave the company entirely. You might need to introduce a new communications process to force employees in complementary but competitive positions to communicate more effectively. The team might need to establish a new approval process to assure that members know about, and have the opportunity to discuss, product or service promises before anyone makes them do it. And when the problem is system-based, you must be willing to stick your neck out by advocating for employees.

These responses build teams and create loyalty among group members as well as toward you (and sometimes even the company). Who wouldn't want to go the extra mile for a manager who at least tries to go the extra mile for you?

The most effective work groups contain complementary, not necessarily similar, personalities and work styles. In such groups, the whole truly becomes more than the sum of its parts. Each person's strengths overlap the other's weaknesses. Creating such a work group is part planning and part luck. It's impossible to know with certainty how people will function together when all you can evaluate is how each one functions separately. Just as mixing chemicals produces different results depending on the substance and its quantity, combining personalities and work styles results in varied effects. Indeed, we often talk about the "chemistry" among group members as critical to the group's success. For better or worse, changing just one member can alter the group far beyond that one member's role and responsibilities.

TAKE ME TO YOUR LEADER

What about you? Shouldn't you be the team's leader? Well, yes and no. You are the leader in that you're the one with the authority to make decisions. Usually, you're also the one held accountable for the group's actions, performance, and productivity. But in most situations, the manager isn't a team member. It's nearly impossible to be a team member and an authority figure simultaneously. Teams function most effectively when there is a relatively even distribution of power, so that each team member feels he or she is making an equitable contribution. As manager, it's your role to stay on the periphery. You need to ensure that everyone knows his or her own role and responsibilities, as well as those of other members. You need to be available to serve the group's needs, whether it is as facilitator, mediator, teacher, mentor, cheerleader, coach, or parent.

When teams are working well together, there is nothing more exciting. But even teams that seem to come together well on their own need guidance and occasionally intervention to help them grow and develop. It's a balancing act that requires constant attention and adjustment. If you as the manager are too involved, then it looks like you're pulling the strings and team members are simply reacting. If you're not involved enough, it's a constant free-for-all. It's natural to feel pride and responsibility for the group's performance. Just remember that this is about the group, not about you.

PROBLEM-SOLVING BASICS

Using a problem-solving approach requires confronting the issues. In fact, for some, a fear of conflict is what gets in the way of resolving it. That fear can stem from a lack of experience, skills, or tools for resolving conflict. Managers in particular need these tools because they must resolve their own conflicts with their staffs, other managers, and outside clients and vendors, as well as help others resolve conflicts.

It's critical that managers differentiate between two types of conflict: unnecessary conflict and resolvable conflict. Sometimes, unnecessary conflicts arise when individuals' perceptions differ or there is a lack of information. Other times, hostile feelings that crop up unexpectedly might cause a disagreement or even build up into a full-blown conflict if signs are not noticed early enough. Resolvable conflict occurs when two individuals' viewpoints on an issue are initially seen as opposing, fixed positions but are actually based on different needs, goals, values, or interests that first need to be understood and then worked out to their mutual satisfaction.

Ten Steps to Successful Conflict Resolution

1. Present the issue without emotion, blame or judgment.

2. Ask for the other person's point of view and listen carefully to her response.

3. Explain your point of view clearly. (Does the other person understand?)

4. Restate the issue, reporting accurately on both parties' needs.

5. Jointly agree upon an objective or condition that satisfies both parties.

6. Brainstorm possible alternative solutions.

7. Evaluate all possible solutions and choose the most viable one.

8. Develop an action plan and record specific assignments, responsibilities, and deadlines.

9. Implement the plan.

10. Evaluate progress, select alternate solutions if needed, and spotlight achievement. (We did it!)

Conflict Resolution Q & A

1. Should conflicts be avoided at all costs in business? Confronting a conflict or tolerating the expression and resolution of differences is generally imperative.

Rather than react impulsively or emotionally, it's critical that you "fight fairly" and ensure conditions are right for engaging in a conflict.

2. How do those engaged in a conflict ensure it will be productive? Everyone must agree to make an effort to resolve the conflict. If one party holds back and decides not to participate, the conflict will escalate to the point of damaging a professional relationship or causing the company some harm.

3. When is the optimal time to confront and resolve a conflict? Consider the amount of time that can realistically be devoted to the process, based on workloads, meetings scheduled, and emotional readiness. For example, are employees too worn and weary to hash things out at day's end?

4. Who should be involved in the conflict resolution? All interested parties should agree upon who will be involved in resolving the conflict. People involved in a conflict don't like to be observed by others unless they mutually decide to enlist the help of a third party who facilitates or mediates the process.

5. Where is the best place to meet? Meet in a neutral space or on some sort of common ground so that it's comfortable for everyone involved. People are less tense discussing conflicts when there are few distractions and listening is easy for everyone.

6. What other considerations should be taken into account? It's critical that people be prepared to air their differences for the most productive outcome, especially if they are not generally friendly or cooperative with each other.

7. If I'm helping others resolve a conflict, what should I do? As long as all parties involved are cooperative, explain the ten-step process and emphasize that your role is to facilitate.

8. As the facilitator, what do I do if the parties don't cooperate and emotions run high? Take everyone through the ten steps without explaining the steps. As you get to each step, identify what each party should do. Ask questions to make sure people understand and agree. It's an effective method although it's time-consuming. Don't permit yourself to be side tracked. Participants attempt to side track the discussion when they don't understand what your method is for helping them.

9. What are some signs that might tell me there is an underlying conflict in my group? People feel safe bringing up certain issues that are, in fact, a mask for the real sources of conflict. At times they aren't aware of the real source of conflict or are not sure of how to bring it up. Typical signs are chronic complaining, increased stress levels, unnecessary competitiveness, absenteeism, failure to accomplish much, retaliation, and demoralizing comments made between or among team members.

10. How do I recognize conflicts early on so I can help to resolve them before they become full-blown arguments? Managers who meet regularly with their staffs—individually and as a team—tend to stay abreast of conflicts. They also learn more about their employees' needs. It's important to develop an active listening style that encourages two-way communication, so differences are brought to the surface easily and quickly, seen as part of the normal process of working together, and resolved as they arise.

Remember:

• Be respectful of the attitudes and beliefs of others when dealing with conflicts of an ethical or moral nature. Conflicts that arise because of beliefs, views, or personal values can only be resolved by respecting other people.

• When both sides have something tangible to bring to the table, compromise can be the fastest and easiest way to resolve differences.

• Negotiating is a method of reaching a compromise settlement. Successful managers will sharpen these skills. Effective negotiating is necessary not only for crisis intervention and conflict management, it's a good skill to have in all aspects of life.

GROUP DYNAMICS: A BALANCING ACT

There are some people who function as human catalysts. They might not seem to be leaders, but somehow more work gets done when they get involved. Watch out for the tendency to evaluate people more on their input (how hard they work, how strong their knowledge is) than on their output (what actually gets accomplished). It's the latter we really value, and we know that the former isn't compatible in every case with actually getting the job done. Some people aren't as skilled on some tasks, yet they somehow make things more cohesive when working in a group environment. Think of it like adding a dash of salt into a soup that's flat. Even though the salt seems minor, somehow, once it's added, the soup suddenly tastes better. Always make sure you have people like this in all of your work groups—they keep things rolling along and get the chemistry flowing.

If you expect to manage future projects that require various team members, put together a skills directory. This way, you can build a list of potential individuals, cross-referencing their names and skills. A skills chart should tell you who does what, indicate how proficient a person is at particular tasks, and, in some cases, provide background information. For example, you might list college or postgraduate degrees next to people's names. You can also learn who might be a good candidate for training in a particular area. Consider adding a column that notes what type of supervisory experience someone has in the event that you need supervisors.

When you sit down with all of the project's key players individually, you might not get an accurate assessment of how well they will interact in a team environment. It's easy for someone to tell you he or she is a team player, but you won't find out for sure until the project gets under way. No ballplayer is going to say, "I hog the ball every opportunity I can," although that might turn out to be the case. In a sample team, Fred might not be the ultimate team player, but if his role is more independent on a daily basis, it might not matter. Also, if he's the only cracker-jack salesperson you've got, you all might have to deal with a little more "attitude" when he's in the office. While you hope everyone on your staff will be gracious, people who are harder to replace are sometimes aware of that and can be more demanding. If you don't have other, more suitable resources, accommodate "difficult" personalities unless they threaten to bring down the whole project.

Learn which members of your team need to be praised often, which members can work contentedly on their own, who needs handholding, and who is a constant challenge. Keep these assessments to yourself—they should never be shared with other members of the team.

In order for group dynamics to function properly, there must be:

- A clear sense of mission and clear goals.

- Mutual respect and an atmosphere of cooperation.

- Ease of communication.

- Ability to resolve conflicts.

- Resources: proper equipment, supplies, and a respected "go-to person" (that's you!).

REWARDING AND SUPPORTING THE TEAM

Motivational strategies often assume an unwarranted degree of similarity among team members. Let's say you decide to motivate people by bringing top performers on stage in front of the company at the monthly "all-hands" meeting, giving them a certificate, followed by a standing ovation from the employees. If you're extroverted and enjoy public recognition, that might sound just fine. But if you're shy and you find your best reward in the work itself, a public ceremony like that might seem more like mortification than motivation. Think carefully about the motivational tools you choose, and avoid the following pitfalls.

NINE MISTAKEN IDEAS ABOUT MOTIVATION

1. "What motivates me motivates others."

2. "People are motivated primarily by money."

3. "Everyone loves to receive formal awards."

4. "Teams are motivated by production quotas."

5. "Cheerleading is a way to get the best from people."

6. "My people are professionals! They don't need 'motivating.'"

7. "I'll think about motivation when there's a problem."

8. "I treat everyone the same in all respects."

9. "Once I know the best way to motivate someone, I'll stick to it without change."

Source: Steven W. Flannes, Ph.D., and Ginger Levin, DPA, *People Skills for Project Managers*, 2001.

The Ten-Penny Challenge

Your ability to influence positive behavioral change in other people is normally higher than you think. It takes patience and regular reinforcement, but it's not dependent particularly on whether you're the official supervisor or not. This strategy implements the famous management mantra, "Catch 'em doing it right!"

Take ten pennies and put them in your pocket. Go out of your office several times a day to look around. Find someone doing something right, and tell the person about it. You don't need to be flowery or overstate the accomplishment; you do need to be specific. When you finish, move one penny into another pocket. Your goal is to move all ten pennies every day. (Save a few for your home life as well.)

Initially, you'll find people resist being praised if they're not used to it. But after a while, you'll find that resistance weakening, and after that, you'll start to see change happening. Give this technique a few months to take hold. Soon, you'll be amazed at how much the people around you are transformed!

PUT OFFICE POLITICS TO GOOD USE

Office politics—who you know, how much you support the ideas and pet projects of your superiors, what relationships you cultivate and which ones you discourage— often play into promotion decisions, at least somewhat. Being a good leader is imperative for all managers, and the ability to schmooze is a part of that. Job skills matter too, of course. But it's important to make sure the right people know your thoughts and see you shine.

This is reality—for you and for your employees. Make sure they each have this same opportunity to showcase successes and achievements for you. Just be sure you know whether that apple-polishing employee is advancing the goals of the team and the company, or simply feeding their own ego. Take the time to ferret out the true objective before you come to a conclusion. When an employee attempts to communicate with you at the expense of the team leader or coworkers, send the employee back to the group to communicate appropriately. Sometimes the employees doing the most communicating have the most time to do so because the real performers are too busy doing the work.

PERSONALITIES AND POLITICS

Relationships form the foundation for effective teams. There is a synergy that exists in the most successful teams, a unique and dynamic blending of individuals and personalities that makes the team as a whole more than just the sum of its parts. The resulting relationships bond people by commonalities (the negative flip side of this is competitive divisions, and sometimes the formation of "enemy camps," within the work group). At this level, what matters is whether people like or dislike each other.

A sort of "relationship language" evolves over time. People learn to get what they want from each other through indirect methods—husbands wait until their wives are in good moods before they tell them that they spent too much money on something, teenage sons mow the lawn and then ask to use the car. In family and social settings outside the work environment, these give-and-take tactics are sometimes viewed as "game playing." In the workplace, we call them office politics. The motivations they reflect are personal—a desire for individual gain, a need for individual attention, a longing for recognition and reward. Because satisfying the motivation often comes at the expense of someone else, we tend to perceive office politics as manipulative and self-serving. Although we all profess to abhor office politics, everyone who works with other people becomes engaged in them to some extent.

At work, everybody wants something—more money, more status, more power, whatever. Some people just want to come in and do a good job. They expect to be recognized, rewarded, and given more responsibility. People are naturally competitive. They might do a good job but still worry that they are not being recognized for their contributions. So they try a bit of manipulation to ensure that others notice their contributions. An employee might drop in on the manager, alone, and casually mention an achievement or ask for advice on something. This self-gratification doesn't usually hurt anyone else, unless the person is taking credit for work someone else did.

A more damaging variation on this theme is the employee who uses the forum of a meeting to ask another employee an embarrassing question. More insidious still is the employee who, "out of sincere dedication and concern," requests a confidential meeting with the manager to point out certain people who are not pulling their share of the workload or who are incompetent, overqualified or in need of remedial help. Then there's the employee who consistently ignores assignments her manager gives her, but gushes, "Gosh, I wish someone had suggested this to me earlier!" when her manager's manager assigns the same project.

Nowadays, technology has given people new ways to polish the apples they want others to notice. An employee can send out a grandstanding e-mail that gives the impression she is managing a project, thereby slighting the team member who really is doing the job. This sort of employee might even "accidentally" copy everyone in the department or, worse, the entire company. E-mail has become the latest weapon in political agendas, replacing drinks after work and standing outside in the rain to grab a smoke as the ideal venue for pitching an idea or kissing shoes. Who gets copied in and who is left off the list is the ultimate political move—checkmate!

THE LAST RESORT: DISCIPLINARY ACTION AND TERMINATION

YOU'VE REACHED THE END of the line with a problem employee, and you're now looking at the door marked Exit. But the story really begins at the door marked Entrance.

If you find yourself asking, "How did we hire this person?" that means it's a perfect time to review hiring practices and make needed improvements. Or, if you're wondering, "Did we do everything possible to resolve attitude and performance issues?" it's frequently more productive to salvage the employee than to dismiss him or her. And, legally speaking, it's imperative that you dot the i's and cross the t's.

As you're preparing to usher someone out the Exit door, you should be aware you're walking on legal eggshells. Firing is a highly regulated action. Even when you think you understand the process perfectly, consult a legal expert. The information presented here is instructive and meant for your consideration. It is not and should not be considered legal advice.

Remember, employees have rights. In most states, you cannot arbitrarily fire an employee. And even if the law doesn't prevent you from doing so, common sense should. The decisions you make regarding an employee's job status—to promote or not, to give a raise or not, to fire or not—are not decisions to make without careful deliberation. Employees (prospective, current, and former) can sue. They can claim you discriminated against them or failed to provide equal opportunity. For your company to defend you and itself against such an allegation requires more than saying, "Well, he just didn't fit in" or "She didn't work hard enough." Those are subjective perceptions that, without quantifiable or subjective substantiation, are nothing more than vague and obscure opinions.

ESSENTIAL CONSIDERATIONS

Few managers, if any, enjoy firing an employee. But, when it's necessary, here are seven points to take into account:

1. Don't take firing lightly. Usually, even a weak job performance can be raised to a satisfactory level. Firing, on the other hand, involves a significant legal risk. It also has a traumatic impact on other members of your staff, even if they understand and appreciate the reasons for the termination.

2. Don't hesitate to consult with counsel. If you have any questions about firing someone, consult with an expert employment attorney prior to the termination. You might save yourself the legal fees of a postfiring lawsuit.

3. Plan what you're going to say. Carefully prepare what you're going to say during a dismissal and stick to it. Otherwise, chances are you'll inadvertently offer kind words regarding work performance. This can lead to legal action. During a firing, you don't want to hint the least bit at anything positive in the person's job performance.

4. Remain calm. Even if the employee you're firing irritates you, keep it to yourself. If he or she lashes out verbally, don't get excited. Soon this person will be gone and will no longer be your problem.

5. Be thoughtful. Treat the employee you're firing as kindly as possible during the termination process. This is usually a very traumatic experience for the individual. Being kind, without conveying anything positive about this person's job performance, can assuage this trauma. It might also decrease the odds that someone will bring a wrongful firing suit against your company or make negative phone calls to your remaining staff.

6. Avoid surprises. Give weak employees every opportunity to improve their work performance or attitude before opting to let them go. If you can prove that you gave them every possible chance, there will be less ammunition for a lawsuit.

Employees who have been aware for some time that their continued employment is on the line will find the actual firing less traumatic. It might well be that they will feel "clued in," and will seek and find employment elsewhere before you can fire them.

At all costs, avoid firing someone who has no idea that his or her job is in jeopardy.

7. Establish a strong paper trail. Good documentation of poor work performance or attitude is essential in defending against a wrongful firing suit. Make a record of any verbal warnings you have given to the employee and, if possible, issue written warnings to him or her well before the firing. Negative performance reviews are a must.

ON THE DOCUMENTATION TRAIL

The first step toward establishing useful documentation is scheduling a meeting. Make it clear to the employee
that it's a meeting for the purpose of job counseling, and
performance issues will be discussed. (These include:
showing up late, leaving early, taking excessively long
lunches, not getting work done on time and flagrantly
violating or ignoring company policies.) While you want
to keep things friendly, this is not a casual chat. It could
be the first step to the end of a job for this employee,
although you hope it's the beginning of the turnaround
you need to see. Follow these guidelines when conducting a job counseling meeting:

• Meet only when you are certain you can remain calm
and professional. If you're angry because the employee's
problems have caused your superiors to come down on
you, give yourself a day or two to cool down.

• Meet somewhere that assures privacy. Your office is
fine if it has floor-to-ceiling walls and a door that closes
(not a cubicle). Otherwise, meet in a conference room or
arrange to use someone else's office.

• Have a clear agenda of what you want to cover, and
put it in writing if that will help you stay on track.

• Establish ground rules: "I will tell you my assessment of your performance for each measure, then give
you an opportunity to share your perspectives and comments. I ask that you not interrupt me, and I promise I
won't interrupt you."

• Have documentation of the problems you want to
discuss—notes, memos, copies of e-mail, work that had
to be redone, or whatever other evidence is relevant.

Be discreet—keep the items in a file folder, not spread out on the desk when the employee arrives.

• Know, at least in general, what you want the employee to do to remedy the situation. Focus on specific and observable behaviors. If you or someone else didn't observe it, it didn't happen. This is not a meeting about feelings or suspicions. It is about actions and behaviors that can be seen, heard, or are otherwise tangible. Cite work that didn't get done, assignments done incorrectly, inappropriate e-mail messages, and so on. Use examples:

  • "Here is the memo you sent to accounts receivable about the Robinson account. It has the wrong balances, and you erroneously flagged the account as past due."

  • "I've gotten complaints from other departments about the number of jokes you forward by e-mail. Here are copies of messages that people have given me."

  • "When we established the timeline for the widgets, you agreed that it was reasonable and would accommodate the kinds of delays that might arise. I've checked with you every week, and you've said you had everything under control. The widget prototype still hasn't been delivered to manufacturing, though the timeline says it should have been in full production six weeks ago."

What if you're dealing with an employee who has a "bad attitude"? You might see this as the crux of the problem, and that could indeed be the case. But you still need tangible evidence—and usually there's an abundance of it: yelling at coworkers, badmouthing others, showing up late and leaving early. Be specific, and provide a few examples.

- "On Tuesday you came in at 9:30 A.M. and you weren't at your desk after 2:30 P.M. On Thursday, you got here at 11 A.M. and I watched you leave at 3:15 P.M."

- "Friday afternoon when Fran asked you to sign off on the department time logs, you told her to get lost. You didn't sign them."

After you've shared your concerns and listened to the employee's perspective, it's time to move into an action mode. Identifying the problems is the first half of your task; identifying solutions is the second. Although you want the employee to participate in developing an improvement plan, you also want to be sure that the plan achieves the goals that are important to you and to the company. Every improvement plan should include these three elements:

1. Specific goals for, and descriptions of, the improvements you want to see. For instance: "Memos that leave this department must be free from grammatical and spelling mistakes."

2. Specific steps for achieving the described improvements: For example: "Run spellchecker just before you save or print any document. For the next two weeks, I want to sit down with you at 11 A.M. and 3 P.M. to review all outgoing memos. We will proof them together."

3. Specific methods for measuring performance and assessing improvement. "I ran spellchecker on these memos that I showed you, and each had at least seven errors. By the end of next week, I want the memos we review together to have fewer than three errors each. In two weeks, I want every memo we review together to have no errors that spellchecker is capable of detecting.

We'll meet again at the end of two weeks to discuss your progress." You are responsible for making sure that follow-up occurs, both in terms of the desired behavior changes as well as the meetings or discussions to monitor or confirm the changes.

The Written Word

It's fine for you to take notes during your meeting— invite the employee to do so as well. Whether you do or not, take another ten or fifteen minutes immediately following the meeting (after the employee leaves) to write down a brief accounting of what transpired.

Be sure to:

• Note which specific examples you used, and how the employee responded.

• Write down the details of the improvement plan you agreed upon, as well as the steps that will be necessary to monitor progress.

• Record any contributing factors from the work environment that the employee feels interfere with productivity, as well as your intentions for addressing issues that involve the employee.

What you do with this documentation depends on your company's policies, the seriousness or complexity of the problem, and your perceptions about how the meeting went. If your company requires or your manager's intuition compels, write a memo to the employee that summarizes the concerns you discussed, the employee's comments and concerns, and the agreement you reached for an improvement plan. To be fair, invite the employee to do the same and be sure that each of you gets copies.

If company policy dictates or if the situation is serious also put copies in the employee's personnel file.

Before you commit your thoughts to writing, consider how your words might sound a few months or years from now, coming from a lawyer's mouth. Be sure your comments are factual and maintain the same tangible focus as your meeting. Laws vary among states, but in many the courts can subpoena any written materials you keep—including notes intended only for your use. If you have any doubts or concerns about what constitutes appropriate documentation, check with your company's HR or legal department.

WHEN COUNSELING FAILS

Most managers hope never to find themselves in the role of disciplinarian. It's uncomfortable for both manager and employee, and nearly always involves other players as well—your superiors, your company's HR department, and sometimes other employees. *Disciplinary action is formal notice (i.e., written warning) that the employee's job is on the line.*

Writing up an employee for poor performance or other problems on the job is a more serious step than counseling, and in most cases should take place only after counseling fails to achieve the desired improvements.

Formally writing up a warning is not the same thing as documenting behavior or conducting counseling meetings. When counseling an employee, your objective is to present the elements of job performance that are unsatisfactory and create a plan for improvement; these are corrective actions that demonstrate you're giving the employee a fair chance to change.

In most situations, if you have not counseled the employee, you will find yourself in hot water if you move directly to disciplinary action. There are exceptions, of course—serious mistakes or actions that jeopardize someone's health or well-being could be grounds for jumping to discipline or even immediate termination. (Hopefully your company has policies and procedures that define these actions; if not, work closely with your HR or legal department to respond appropriately.) There could come a point at which you need to suggest the employee find work elsewhere and ask for a voluntary resignation, or you might eventually have to fire the employee.

Many managers are leery of committing adverse performance reports to writing, for fear that what they say will come back to bite them in court. However, attorneys who specialize in employment law generally believe documentation is a company's best safeguard against frivolous lawsuits. Written job descriptions and performance appraisals establish procedural consistency. The paper trail that is likely to cause trouble is the one built solely for the purpose of carrying out a particular action. Documentation should support decisions, not create them.

FIRING AN EMPLOYEE

No manager enjoys the prospect of firing an employee. Firing someone is the most serious consequence for failing to improve. Before you come to the decision that you need to end a person's employment, you must be sure in your heart of hearts that this is the right thing to do. Then you must be sure that you have complied with all relevant laws, regulations, and company policies, and that all of the paperwork is completely in order. Remember, there are laws that govern firing, even in fire-at-will states. This is a decision from which there is no turning back.

A SHORT OVERVIEW

When you are ready to proceed with the termination, call the employee into your office. Approach him or her by saying you have something to discuss. After the employee and any other managerial personnel or witnesses have gathered in your office, get to the point quickly. Briefly explain to the employee that he or she is being fired. Summarize the main reasons for dismissal; recap the warnings that have been issued; and cite the opportunities extended to improve his or her performance record. Give the person a check for monies due. If you are offering severance pay, detail the severance offer and present the employee with the forfeiture document to be signed if the severance is to be paid. Explain any continued work options. Allow the employee to clean out his or her office or desk immediately, or offer to mail personal belongings later. If the employee elects to have you mail his or her belongings, have two people oversee the cleaning process to be sure that all of the employee's personal possessions are mailed.

Show appropriate sympathy for the employee, but not empathy. Do not waiver or change your mind. Do not overstate any aspect of the employee's performance.

Be open in communicating with the employee, but do not compromise your position.

Plan the meeting to fire the employee according to your company's policies and procedures. Some managers prefer to conduct a firing at the end of the workday, so the employee can collect his or her things and leave without everyone else watching. Will a security guard have to escort the fired employee back to the office to gather his or her possessions and then out of the building? Does an HR representative supervise the packing?

As humiliating as these requirements might seem, they are often necessary safeguards for the company to prevent theft or sabotage. If the employee has valued work saved on the company's computer network or on a company computer, back up all the files the night before you intend to fire the employee as additional protection. Before the meeting, rehearse what you intend to say. When you do meet with the employee:

• Have an HR representative or your superior present as well. This bolsters your authority and lessens the likelihood of emotional pleas or outbursts.

• Keep the conversation short, to the point, and unemotional. (See the end of this chapter for an example.)

• Review the conversations and documentation that support the decision to fire the employee. It is not necessary or advisable to invite the employee's comments or perspective. The time for that is long past.

Expect the meeting to become emotional, certainly for the employee and probably for you. Regardless of the reasons for the firing, this person is someone you know. Be prepared to deal with the gamut of emotion, from anger and sadness to pleading and tears. You might need to sit in the room with the employee until he or she regains composure.

If you've done your job as a manager, the firing shouldn't come as a total shock to the employee (although the finality of it might be temporarily stunning). You've counseled the employee about his or her performance issues or whatever other problems that have led up to the firing, and you've given the employee plenty of opportunities to fix them. Keep your cool and stick to the "script" you've rehearsed. If it is necessary for someone to escort the fired employee from the premises, be sure that person is ready and waiting.

As soon as possible after the terminated employee has gone, assemble the other members of the team to give them the news. Keep the reasons for the employee's termination to yourself; such information is confidential. Chances are, the other team members knew this was coming and they know better than you do why this was the only option. Sometimes, however, you need to reassure other employees that this was a matter specific to the fired employee; it's natural for them to feel some fear and apprehension about the security of their own jobs. Other employees might want to talk about how they feel, but it's generally better to focus on how duties will be reassigned, what the plans are for hiring a replacement, and other such details. The key is to move on. It's important to treat people with respect after they've been fired, regardless of the reasons for firing them. Those who remain will watch how you handle things, and their perceptions will affect their attitudes and performance.

SEVERANCE

First, by law, you immediately need to remunerate a terminated employee for any unused vacation or personal time, all regular and overtime hours worked, previously unpaid, earned bonuses, and any other outstanding pay.

When you fire an employee, you should pay severance for any just cause short of confiscating the queen's jewels, even if he or she has only been with you for ninety days or less. It is decent, remaining employees expect you to do it, and it makes you look better in the worst of situations.

Many firms that pay severance offer two weeks pay. Others pay two weeks plus one week for each year of service the employee has given to the company. Still others are considerably more generous, particularly to employees who held senior positions. In this case, six months' to a year's pay is not atypical and is predicated on the assumption that a senior-level employee will have a more difficult time obtaining a new and equal job than will an entry-level employee.

Paying the employee severance is not only proper but may circumvent lawsuits later on. Whatever you decide to do regarding severance pay, in all termination situations, severance for similar positions with similar service time should be consistent. If you continually change your severance policies, you are only adding to your legal risks.

You should only pay severance, however, if the employee agrees to sign a document that forfeits her right to sue you for wrongful termination. Don't be cheap in this lion's pit of potential danger. Have a lawyer draw up the release document so that it is, as much as possible, bullet proof. You should give the employee twenty-four hours to review, sign, and return the document to you, otherwise it might not hold up in court should the employee decide to sue you anyway. If the employee is age forty or over you may have to grant the person a number of days to review such a document.

Be aware of how to handle reference calls for a former fired, employee. If you give out any information on such an employee, other than dates of employment and a salary confirmation, you risk a lawsuit. There was even an instance where a company lost a suit brought by a terminated employee because a good reference was supplied but the employee felt, and the jury agreed, that the reference wasn't good enough! Once there's no turning back and you must terminate an employee, be smart, and always protect yourself and your company's interests!

AN EMPLOYEE TERMINATION SCENARIO

The following dialog provides an excerpt from a firing that involves an employee who had sincerely tried to do his job but just hadn't been able to perform at a satisfactory level. Note how the manager shows patience and expresses sympathy but does not offer false praise or waiver in his decision. Remember that when terminating an employee, having another manager present reduces the risk of hostile confrontation. If the firing does not go smoothly, the second manager can be called upon, as a witness should any legal action ensue at some later point.

Manager: Tom, please have a seat.

Tom: Thank you.

Manager: Tom, I know that you have tried hard to succeed at your job. Nonetheless, for some months now, your overall performance has not been satisfactory. There are too many errors in the accounts payable reports and your attempts to check each report carefully have slowed down the pace of your work considerably. We cannot retain you in this position and we must let you go.

Tom: Do you mean I'm fired?

Manager: Yes, that is correct. I'm very sorry that this didn't work out.

Tom: I know I can do the job. Give me another chance. I really like working here.

Manager: Tom, we have given you at least two written warnings and several verbal warnings.

Tom: But my supervisor says the quality of my work is improving.

Manager: While the number of errors has decreased, the quality is still not satisfactory. And in working to decrease the amount of errors your work pace has become unsatisfactory. I know you've tried . . . but it's still not working out.

Tom: What about another position? I've never really liked payables. How about the entry-level position in accounts receivable? I'll really give it my all.

Manager: Tom, it's time to move on. We all like you here. This is a difficult decision for all of us. But the decision has been made. We truly wish you the best.

POWERFUL COMMUNICATION SKILLS STAY WITH YOU

SHOW ME A SUCCESSFUL MANAGER, and I'll show you a successful communicator. As you move up the rungs of the corporate ladder from entry-level management into higher-level positions, you're perfecting your communication skills. That's a given! Don't treat your evolving communication skills haphazardly. If you acknowledge the need for good communication skills early in your career and develop those skills purposefully, there will be little that's left to chance regarding your success as a manager and your own personal career growth. No matter whether you set your sights on the stars or just a tad below, remember: *You can't get there from here* without good, better, and best communication skills. These include:

- **Conversing:** Talk *and* listen.

- **Reading and comprehending:** Pay attention to more than just the words; understand the message.

- **Writing:** Commit your ideas to print, and keep messages short, sweet, and clear.

- **Coaching:** Teach, train, and strive to help your staff improve.

• **Mentoring:** Be an adviser, and act as a sounding board.

• **Negotiating:** Work to bring two "divided" parties to the same place.

• **Compromising:** Give a little, take a little.

• **Motivating:** Fill employees with enthusiasm, and point out what's in it for them.

• **Disciplining:** Put a stop to unacceptable behavior by introducing consequences.

• **Instructing:** Introducing and explaining all new information.

• **Dismissing:** Escorting someone to and through a Permanent Exit Door when necessary.

This small volume has already touched on all of these communication skills, with the exception of the second point on the list. Reading and comprehending is indeed a communication skill. The writer attempts to impart information to you but nothing happens until you make an effort to receive it. So before you reach the last page of this book, take a moment to focus on the importance of reading and comprehending.

COMPANY POLICIES AND PROCEDURES

Policies define a company's responsibilities and obligations to employees and vice versa. They also reflect a company's responsibilities and obligations to its customers. Policies exist for both legal and practical purposes. Some policies explain how a company complies with certain laws and regulations. Others delineate procedures and expectations. In most situations, you inherit these policies in the form of written communication, and you must comply with and enforce them.

In order to abide by company policies, you must take the time to read and understand them. When was the last time you read a written company policy? If you're like many managers, you can't remember when. Moreover, you might find them difficult to understand, which isn't necessarily a reflection on your comprehension skills. Although often, written policies as well as state laws and regulations seem filled with complicated jargon and confusing mumbo jumbo, most employment laws and company policies are in place to define and ensure fairness in the ways the company treats its employees. Most people agree that everyone should have the same opportunities to pursue their interests and aptitudes. When you're managing people it's essential to treat them fairly. Admittedly, though, one person's concept of fairness is not exactly the next person's concept of fairness. So it follows that you should rely upon policies and related written documents to provide guidance. But it's all to no avail if you don't read this material.

It's your responsibility as a manager to be familiar with the laws and regulations that apply in your state and industry, and to your company. *Not knowing is no excuse*.

If you don't know your state's employment laws and regulations, look into one of the many professional organizations that sponsor workshops and seminars about employment laws and related issues. The important thing is to be familiar with these laws and stay up to date on any changes. And, if company policies, procedures, and other related documents (for instance, job descriptions and forms) are outdated or unclear, take steps to bring about change.

OTHER RELATED DOCUMENTS

Forms are valuable communication tools. Experts suggest that companies wouldn't survive without forms and documentation. Does your company have a forms policy? Does it provide that forms be updated periodically to meet needs?

Entire books are written to serve as guides for perfecting company policies, procedures, and forms. If you're not using forms in your department, should you be using them? Generic forms are available, but they often don't provide the appropriate level of detail. In many large companies, the Human Resources department employs policies and procedures staff to help executives originate and update these documents. Smaller foundations and other organizations hire consultants who specialize in writing these materials. You can go to the Internet for information as needed. For example, browse HRTools.com, *www.hrtools.com*. This online resource offers extensive information about all aspects of human resources, including a wide variety of standard forms that can be downloaded. And don't be afraid to poke around the Internet to find other options. Internet search engines such as Google (*www.google.com*) and Yahoo (*www.yahoo.com*) can help you locate a great variety of resources. The Web sites mentioned in this book are just a few examples.

STAYING INFORMED

You call upon your reading and comprehending skills daily when you must discriminate and select and read only the written material (for example, newspapers, industry information, and special reports) that is pertinent to your needs. If you're slow to read and comprehend, you'll take in new information slowly. Since there are only so many hours in a day, you'll read less than the next manager. You might miss something important—something that affects your employees, your industry, or yourself directly.

You might want to search for and subscribe to business newsletters that focus on the information you need. These letters often boil down extraneous material and highlight precisely what the manager needs to know. Moreover, a group of editors is charged with delivering the information in an easy-to-read and understandable format. Today a good deal of that kind of information is available online. For example, "Industry Standard" is a publication that covers the Internet economy, including news, analysis, and new products and services. Industry Standard's online version is available at *www.thestandard.com*, and a print edition is available by subscription (forty-eight issues a year). It's possible to subscribe online.

You can obtain information about workplace safety and health, including injury prevention suggestions, OSHA requirements, and inspections and compliance, by accessing *www.osha.gov*. Additionally, *www.sbaonline. sba.gov*, the United States Small Business Administration site, contains a potpourri of useful information for small and family businesses.

Check company policy regarding Internet use for acquiring information pertinent to your job. If there isn't any policy, write one, or ask that one be established and documented.

Even though you'll frequently rely upon company experts (e.g., attorneys) to map out plans of action, you'll become a more valuable company employee when you make it your business to be generally well informed regarding all company-related matters. Reading and comprehending makes it possible every time!

WHAT ORGANIZATIONS EXPECT FROM MANAGERS

Consistency. Consistency. Consistency. As a manager, you are the face of your company. You represent upper management to your employees and you're expected to:

- Reflect and support company goals and objectives.

- Reflect and support company policies and procedures.

- Convey the company's needs to employees.

- Give upper management feedback about how employees perceive and respond to company goals and policies.

- Give upper management feedback about what works and what doesn't regarding how the company does business.

To be consistent and effective in supporting a company's principles, managers must also be committed to them. If you deeply resent certain policies or goals, this commitment will be difficult for you. Ask yourself:

- What is it, precisely, that I don't like?

- Why do I feel strongly about it?

- Do other managers share my feelings?

- What have I done to attempt to change the policy or goal?

- Could I live with this policy or goal if I understood the reason it's in place?

Often, simply exploring the reasons for your feelings brings your concerns to the surface. Then you can examine them and decide if they truly have merit. Sometimes, how we feel about certain policies or goals has little to do with the principle, but instead relates back to some personal experience for which we're still "carrying baggage." If you think about it, companies don't have anything to gain by implementing policies and procedures that are unreasonable. Sometimes the original purpose for the guideline gets lost in the approval process. Once someone points this out, it's possible to correct flaws.

Successful companies create working environments in which employees and managers feel welcome to share their views and concerns. This kind of dialog helps companies avert potential problems. After all, the company doesn't exist solely for the purpose of creating rules. Rules are in place to support the company's mission and goals, whatever those are. Like nearly all other dimensions of doing business, rules must be dynamic to remain effective. This means that a company must continually review and reassess its policies, to be sure the policies are keeping up with the changes in the business environment.

As a manager, it's your role to facilitate the process. But you'll never be able to accomplish any of the above goals without excellent communication skills.

PRIORITIZING: THERE'S SO MUCH TO DO!

Every company, regardless of its products and services, requires a certain amount of structure. Some functions and departments, such as accounting, are bound to established procedures for conducting their work. People who work in these areas generally (but not always) have work styles and personalities that are compatible with this level of structure. Other functions and departments require structure that supports project timelines and productivity goals. Such structure might be vague and variable, or fairly rigid, depending on the work and the employees doing it. Structure might require you to:

- Establish priorities.

- Identify tasks.

- Identify goals.

- Indicate whether tasks are daily, weekly, or monthly.

- Suggest the time of day and the amount of time the employee should work on each task or specified tasks.

Remember, the backbone of structure is clear communication!

As a manager, you need to help employees who need structure learn how to prioritize. Once the base structure of priorities is in place, most employees can then build additional structure around those priorities. Generally, it's most effective to meet with employees one-on-one, so you can gauge just how much structure each individual employee needs.

- Identify specific tasks that must be accomplished by day's end.

- Be sure the employee has the tools and know-how required to complete tasks.

- Identify common problems that might arise.

- Establish a procedure for dealing with those problems.

- Use charts or diagrams if practical. Or, ask the employee to take notes.

- Meet with the employee at the end of the day to assess results.

• Establish procedures for unexpected emergencies or changes in priorities.

• In time, let the employee set his/her priorities with less monitoring from you.

• Be an excellent role model. Show how you prioritize your day.

• Follow up to see what works daily/weekly and what doesn't work.

Think about the various personality types you manage. For example, does the procrastinator immediately leap into your thoughts here? Even the social butterfly could be "brought down to Earth" with a good dose of structure and a few lessons on prioritizing. Then, there's the rookie, who might not be experienced enough to know how to set priorities properly all the time. He or she would surely be favorably impacted, too, if you used some of these techniques. Similarly, the other negaholics discussed earlier in this book might all focus more on improving their work skills if you "sold" them on prioritizing. It's a suggestion worth considering.

Sometimes, an employee's apparent inability to prioritize reflects an overwhelming workload rather than a structure problem. If this is the case, it's all the more important that you get the message as soon as possible.

Over and over again, your ability to communicate efficiently and effectively must remain in high gear. The more you exercise this enviable skill, the more valuable you are in the workplace and everywhere you go.

A COMPANY SPOKESPERSON: WHO, ME?

When you attend tradeshows, participate at professional organizations' meetings (your local chamber of commerce, for instance), or serve on community committees (for example, a local hospital fundraising committee), you might not think about it, but what you do and how you do it reflects upon your company. You'll utilize all the communication skills you sharpen when you're working with employees, management, vendors, customers, and clients. These skills readily translate to any environment in which you find yourself. Of course, you'll use these skills when dealing with family members and friends, too. You simply don't leave them behind when you leave your office at the end of the business day. Excellent communication skills become a part of you and greatly enhance your positive image. Just imagine your staff members making similar comments about you because of the strong impact your good communication skills have had on their work situations:

- "Jon is such a nice person. He makes me feel important because he always takes the time to listen to me."

- "Sara is an excellent coach. I never thought I could learn that new software program but she made it easy for me."

- "Michael is a terrific 'go-to' guy. When I asked him about the new Forms policy, he was completely familiar with it and helped me to understand it."

- "Christina made me realize I should transfer departments. It never occurred to me that my 'people skills' were better suited to sales than to systems. I love the new work and just earned a big bonus!"

Fear of Public Speaking

Managers usually have to speak to groups of people. Remarks might be addressed to a small gathering of team members or an auditorium filled with people. Although some people do enjoy the spotlight, most go on record as "preferring to die" rather than getting up in front of a large group of people to speak. Even if you experience tremendous anxiety when it comes to public speaking, know that with practice, you can build confidence and overcome this fear.

Being a Company Spokesperson

Does your company have an official company spokesperson policy? Don't assume you can speak to reporters or others who plan to disseminate your comments to the public. Usually, this task is reserved for a highly placed company official or a public relations director. If not, and you have a knack for it, you might ultimately be well known as an excellent off-the-cuff speaker and be granted official company spokesperson status.

Danny Lanier, in his book, *Setting the Pace for Business Success*, recalls how he was sure he couldn't speak on a stage in front of an audience. Eventually, Danny built up his ability to the point where he could speak to large audiences made up of business people from many countries. Danny's comments were even translated into the appropriate languages and some attendees used headphones to receive Danny's message. Can you imagine talking to large audiences made up of people of different cultural backgrounds and delivering a meaningful and well appreciated speech to all assembled? Danny tells his readers, "If I can do it, anyone can do it!"

How Good It Is to Be in Control!

A few years ago, the concept of empowering employees to act began to be widely touted. Give your employees permission to act, give them the tools to act, instill confidence in employees, and step back. It's also critical to make two-way communication channels readily available. These include:

- Intranets

- Message boards

- Online chat rooms

- Videoconferencing

- Open-door policy

- Meetings

And keep your finger on the collective pulse.

Your company may or may not empower employees. It's "right" for some businesses and "not right" for others. Business pundits will probably examine the phenomenon for years to come since this strategy has pros and cons. It does, however, appear to be a trend. Moreover, it could be the best management style to come down the pike in a long time. If so, it's here to stay.

But enough about empowering others. What about empowering you?

When you feel as though you're at the top of your game, there's nothing you can't achieve. That's an exhilarating way to approach each business day. Sharpen your communication skills and, conservatively speaking, half the battle is won.

Consider this scenario:

Jeannette felt frustrated when two negaholics were assigned to her department. Alan was a bully and Janis was a social butterfly. Jeannette heard this from a colleague in the building and she didn't doubt this manager's assessment. As the weeks passed, Jeannette reached into her bag-of-tricks and tried to mold, shape, or deflect the negaholics' damaging behavior. She noticed, however, that when she left the office most days she felt exhausted. At least one morning a week she seriously entertained the notion of calling in sick. "What's wrong with me?" she asked herself. "When did I start to lose it?" When she realized that the negaholics' arrival coincided with her distress, she decided to speak with her own boss. In the four years she had been with the company, she never shirked a responsibility. She never said "no" to any assignment. But she was going to say "no" to keeping the bully and the social butterfly in her department.

When she left her boss's office, she literally discovered what it felt like to have a great weight lifted from her shoulders. The bully and the social butterfly would be transferred by month's end.

Two months later, Jeannette was offered a new management position where she would be overseeing a staff of eighty people. This represented almost twice the number she had managed before. She was thrilled with the offer and accepted the job.

"What's right with me?" she asked herself. "When did I step into the fast lane for promotion?" She thought about it for a long time. "Maybe I'll never know," she conceded. And then one day she recognized the offer might have been tied to her response to the negaholics. She said "no" to the boss—something she had never done before. Jeannette knew she had used all the ammunition in her manager's arsenal to making Janis and Al productive members of the department. When she realized that wasn't to be, however, she demonstrated that she could hold her ground, be assertive, say "no," and mean it. As a capable manager with strong communication skills, she had come full circle.

GOING UP

You've just taken quite an elevator ride! When you started to read this book, you were on the ground floor. Now, at the end of the book, you're on the top floor. This little resource contains some "big" concepts. You've probably been exposed to many of these "truths" before, but now that you've read these pages and the messages have had time to sink in, you have a firmer grasp of how to handle difficult people. Hopefully, you've enjoyed the ride and you'll step off the elevator knowing your journey to the top of your game is not only possible, it's not even difficult. Managing tough employees and handling difficult work situations is something you can—and will—do.

Index

A

absence, leaves of, 16
agendas, employee, 31
anger, 36
appraisals, employee, 36–41
assertiveness, 28–29
attitudes
    of bullies, 48–51
    of know-it-alls, 78–79, 82–85
    managers', and employee
      performance, 3–16
    of "no people skills" person,
      108–13
    of overly-sensitive people,
      126–29
    of procrastinators, 70–71
    of silent types, 90–94
    of social butterflies, 99–103
    unapproachable, 111–13
    of whiners, 58–59

B

behaviors
    anticipating, 32–33
    assessing different, 31–41
    of bullies, 46–48, 51–52
    of know-it-alls, 75–78, 79–82
    of manipulators, 132–37
    of "no people skills" person,
      106–7
    of overly-sensitive people,
      124–25

    of procrastinators, 66–70
    of rookies, 116–19
    of silent types, 87–90
    of social butterflies, 95–98
    of whiners, 56–58, 60–62
body language, 145–48
bullies, 32, 45–53

C

CEO, mood of, 150
common sense, 7
communication
    art of effective, 141–58
    body language, 145–48
    channels, 204
    company policies/procedures
      for, 194–96
    components of good, 141–45
    constructive criticism, 152–56
    importance of, 193–94, 201,
      202
    issues, tips for resolving,
      156–58
    keeping open, 35
    listening skills, 142–44
    nonverbal, 145–48
    open-door policy, 151–52
    public speaking skills, 203–4
    reading comprehension skills,
      194–97
    skills, 7, 25–27
    small talk, 148–50
    writing skills, 144–45